GREAT MYSTERIES

President Truman and the Atomic Bomb

OPPOSING VIEWPOINTS®

Look for these and other exciting *Great Mysteries: Opposing Viewpoints* books:

GREAT MYSTERIES

President Truman and the Atomic Bomb

OPPOSING VIEWPOINTS®

by Michael O'Neal

Greenhaven Press, Inc.   P.O. Box 289009, San Diego, California 92198-0009

P G

Library of Congress Cataloging-in-Publication Data

O'Neal, Michael, 1949-
  President Truman and the atomic bomb : opposing viewpoints / by Michael O'Neal.
    p. cm. — (Great mysteries)
  Includes bibliographical references.
  Summary: Discusses the events and decisions that led to the bombing of Hiroshima in 1945, particularly Truman's role as decision maker and initiator of the act.
  ISBN 0-89908-079-0
  1. Truman, Harry S., 1884-1972—Military leadership—Juvenile literature. 2. Atomic bomb—History—Juvenile literature. 3. Hiroshima-shi (Japan)—History—Bombardment, 1945—Juvenile literature. [1. Atomic bomb—History. 2. Hiroshima-shi (Japan)—Bombardment, 1945. 3. Truman, Harry S., 1884-1972.] I. Title. II. Series: Great mysteries (Saint Paul, Minn.)
E814.053 1990
973.918'092—dc20   90-35611
  [B]   CIP
                                                               AC

*To Libby and Marc
in the hope that your generation
will find a way
to beat these swords
into plowshares*

"Great events have happened. The world is changed and it is time for sober thought."

Henry Stimson, President Truman's secretary of war

Contents

Introduction

This book is written for the curious—those who want to explore the mysteries that are everywhere. To be human is to be constantly surrounded by wonderment. How do birds fly? Are ghosts real? Can animals and people communicate? Was King Arthur a real person or a myth? Why did Amelia Earhart disappear? Did history really happen the way we think it did? Where did the world come from? Where is it going?

Great Mysteries: Opposing Viewpoints books are intended to offer the reader an opportunity to explore some of the many mysteries that both trouble and intrigue us. For the span of each book, we want the reader to feel that he or she is a scientist investigating the extinction of the dinosaurs, an archaeologist searching for clues to the origin of the great Egyptian pyramids, a psychic detective testing the existence of ESP.

One thing all mysteries have in common is that there is no ready answer. Often there are *many* answers but none on which even the majority of authorities agrees. *Great Mysteries: Opposing Viewpoints* books introduce the intriguing views of the experts, allowing the reader to participate in their explorations, their theories, and their disagreements as they try to explain the mysteries of our world.

But most readers won't want to stop here. These *Great Mysteries: Opposing Viewpoints* aim to stimulate the reader's curiosity. Although truth is often impossible to discover, the search is fascinating. It is up to the reader to examine the evidence, to decide whether the answer is there—or to explore further.

"Penetrating so many secrets, we cease to believe in the unknowable. But there it sits nevertheless, calmly licking its chops."

H.L. Mencken, American essayist

Prologue

Secrets and Mysteries

On April 25, 1945, a car pulled up to the White House in Washington, D.C. Two men emerged from the car. One was Sec. of War Henry Stimson. The other was Gen. Leslie Groves. The two men had an appointment with Pres. Harry S. Truman to discuss a matter that would have a major influence on the course of World War II.

A Secret Meeting?

There was nothing unusual about Secretary Stimson meeting with the president. As an important member of Truman's cabinet, Stimson had frequently conferred with Truman during the two weeks since Truman took office. But Groves's appearance at the White House seemed to be another matter. In fact, Groves's visit was a closely guarded secret. Only later was it learned that while Stimson entered Truman's office through the usual door, Groves slipped in unseen through a side door. Even Truman's appointment secretary did not know of his presence.

General Groves carried with him a report that he was giving to the president at the request of Stimson. He presented the report, and after some discussion, he and Stimson left as quietly as they had come.

(opposite page) The authorization to drop atomic bombs on Hiroshima and Nagasaki led to economic ruin and nuclear devastation.

No objection to
declassification
by AFSWP
[signature]
Hd C.C.

18 June 1948

WAR DEPARTMENT
OFFICE OF THE CHIEF OF STAFF
WASHINGTON 25, D. C.

25 July 1945

TO: General Carl Spaats
Commanding General
United States Army Strategic Air Forces

1. The 509 Composite Group, 20th Air Force will
deliver its first special bomb as soon as weather will
permit visual bombing after about 3 August 1945 on one of the
targets: Hiroshima, Kokura, Niigata and Nagasaki. To
carry military and civilian scientific personnel from the
War Department to observe and record the effects of the
explosion of the bomb, additional aircraft will accompany
the airplane carrying the bomb. The observing planes will
stay several miles distant from the point of impact of the
bomb.

2. Additional bombs will be delivered on the above
targets as soon as made ready by the project staff. Further
instructions will be issued concerning targets other than
those listed above.

3. Dissemination of any and all information concerning
the use of the weapon against Japan is reserved to the
Secretary of War and the President of the United States.
No communiques on the subject or releases of information
will be issued by Commanders in the field without specific
prior authority. Any news stories will be sent to the War
Department for special clearance.

4. The foregoing directive is issued to you by direc-
tion and with the approval of the Secretary of War and of
the Chief of Staff, USA. It is desired that you personally
deliver one copy of this directive to General MacArthur and
one copy to Admiral Nimitz for their information.

[signature] Thos T Handy
THOS. T. HANDY
General, G.S.C.
Acting Chief of Staff

What purpose did Groves and Stimson have in meeting with the president? What was in Groves's report? What did he tell the president that was so important? And why did they need to meet in such a secretive way?

Potsdam

On July 16 of the same year, in the German city of Potsdam, just outside Berlin, President Truman met with two other men. This meeting was no secret; he was holding a conference with British Prime Minister Winston Churchill and Soviet Premier Joseph Stalin. The three leaders were meeting to discuss policies connected with the end of the war in Europe and with the ongoing war against Japan in the Pacific.

On the evening of the sixteenth, Truman was handed a cabled message. The message came from an air base in New Mexico called Alamogordo. Ac-

During the 1945 Potsdam Conference, British Prime Minister Winston Churchill, U.S. Pres. Harry Truman, and Soviet leader Joseph Stalin discuss policies to end the war with Japan.

cording to Stimson, who was with Truman, the president seemed to have been nervously waiting for this message. He scanned its contents eagerly. The message read: "Operated on this morning. Diagnosis not yet complete but results seem satisfactory and already exceed expectations." Truman seemed elated.

No one among Truman's family and friends was ill. No one had been operated on. So what was the meaning of this strange telegram? What was the "operation" the message referred to? And why was the president so pleased?

The *Enola Gay* touches down after dropping its deadly cargo on Hiroshima. The *Enola Gay* was piloted by Col. Paul Tibbets, who named the bomber after his mother.

Tinian Island

Later that same month, the ship *Indianapolis* arrived at the tiny island of Tinian in the western Pacific. The ship was lucky to reach its destination. Japanese bombers were patrolling this area of the Pacific, looking for American ships. But the *Indianapolis* managed to slip through. It docked at Tinian just long enough for its top secret cargo to be taken out of the hold. Just a few days after the ship left the island, Japanese patrols spotted it, attacked, and sank the *Indianapolis*. We can only wonder:

Would history have been different if the ship had been struck before making its mysterious delivery?

Stationed on Tinian was a small band of pilots and technicians. Their mission was to deliver a knockout punch against Japan and finally bring the long war in the Pacific to an end. The arrival of the *Indianapolis* signaled an end to their wait. Within days, the strike orders were posted on the bulletin board. At first glance, they seemed ordinary. They told the pilots what planes to use, how many gallons of fuel to put in them, even when their crews should eat breakfast on the day of the mission. Everything that had to be loaded into the plane was accounted for, right down to the very last item—"Bomb: Special."

On August 5, 1945, that "Bomb: Special" was loaded into the bay of a B-29 bomber. The bomber was called the *Enola Gay*, named after the mother of its commander, Col. Paul Tibbets. Early in the morn-

The *Indianapolis* carries top-secret cargo to the island of Tinian. After its mysterious delivery, the ship was attacked by Japanese patrols.

ing of the sixth, the plane took off on its mission, bearing its terrifying cargo to its final destination.

At 8:15 that cargo was dropped into the soft morning air over the Japanese city of Hiroshima, and the world has never been the same since.

Questions

What is the connection between these three events which took place thousands of miles from one another in the closing months of World War II? Since 1945 historians have been trying to understand that connection. Many questions about these events remain unanswered. Only one thing is known for certain: They were steps in the weightiest, most terrible decision that any American president has ever had to make.

One

The Decision That Changed the World

Earlier in the morning of August 6, air raid sirens had sounded throughout the city of Hiroshima. Residents took cover, but nothing happened. This was not the first time that an expected attack by American bombers had failed to occur. So the people of Hiroshima went about their morning's business.

When air raid sirens sounded again shortly after eight o'clock, many people in the city remained unconcerned, thinking that it was just another false alarm. For some people, work in the factories had just started. Homemakers were planning their day's errands, and school for most of the city's children had just begun. The few people who were outdoors, or who happened to be looking out a window, were pleased to see a parachute drifting slowly to earth—the usual sign that an American bomber had been hit by antiaircraft fire, forcing its pilot to parachute to safety.

But what most of these people never learned was that dangling from the end of this parachute was an atomic bomb—the first bomb of this type that had ever been used in warfare. At an altitude of just under two thousand feet, the bomb detonated. With a flash of light, Hiroshima lay in ruins, blasted

(opposite page) An aerial map of Hiroshima targets the landing site of the devastating atomic bomb.

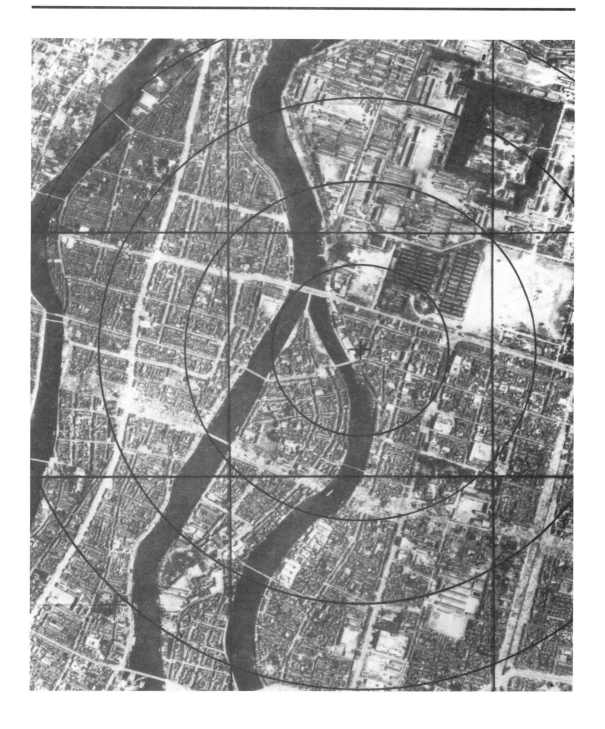

beyond recognition. Destruction on this scale had never been seen in war—and has never been seen since. In seconds, an area one mile across was utterly destroyed. Not a single building was left even partially standing as a result of the explosion—an explosion whose force was that of over twenty-four million pounds of dynamite.

Firestorm

The destructive effects of the bomb did not stop with the initial blast. Within moments a tremendous firestorm began to consume everything within hundreds of yards of the blast. This firestorm created a ball of heat so intense that fires sprang up as far as

The atomic bomb's mighty blast leaves Hiroshima in ruins. Once a prosperous and bustling city, Hiroshima was reduced to burned rubble in a matter of moments.

two miles from the center of the explosion. The intense heat carried soot and debris skyward, creating the "mushroom cloud" characteristic of atomic explosions. By evening an ashy "black rain" was falling on the city, leaving ugly stains on everything it touched.

Overshadowing the complete destruction of the city was the loss of human life. Eighty-thousand people were killed almost instantly by the initial blast. Another 100,000 were seriously injured, many of them badly burned. Thousands of survivors wandered about the devastated city, dazed, searching for friends and relatives and seeking medical help for their injuries. What the survivors did not know was that their bodies had been invaded by radioactivity. For days, months, and even years, this radioactivity would cause a legacy of stillbirths, birth defects, cancer, and other diseases. Harder to measure was the sense of loss and despair among the survivors, leading many to believe that those who had been quickly killed were the lucky ones.

Three days later the city of Nagasaki met a similar fate, at a cost of over forty thousand lives. Faced with the savage destructiveness of the atomic bomb, the Japanese government—at war with the United States since 1941—surrendered, bringing World War II to an end. The atomic bomb had done what was promised, but on a scale that no one had ever imagined.

Developing the Bomb

The dropping of the atomic bomb on Japan was one of the most dramatic events of the twentieth century. But the story behind the invention and development of the bomb has its own drama, too. That story began in the 1920s and 1930s when scientists proved that the atom could be split, releasing the energy that holds it together. Soon, scientists began to ask whether atomic "chain reactions"—the pro-

"No man, in our position and subject to our responsibilities, holding in his hand a weapon of such possibilities [as the atomic bomb] could have failed to use it and afterwards looked his countrymen in the face."

Henry Stimson, President Truman's secretary of war

"My own feeling is that in being the first to use it, we had adopted an ethical standard common to the barbarians of the dark ages."

Adm. William Leahy, President Truman's chief of staff

Three days after the bombing of Hiroshima, the U.S. blasts Nagasaki. Wreckage is piled high, testifying to the unimaginable power of the atomic bomb.

cess of splitting countless millions of atoms—could release energy that would be a source of heat and power.

World War II

In September 1939, World War II began when Germany invaded Poland. American involvement in the war began on December 7, 1941, when Japanese bombers attacked the American fleet at Pearl Harbor, a naval base in Hawaii. Soon, American forces were involved in a war on two fronts, one in Europe, the other in the Pacific. As the war dragged on and more and more American lives were lost, scientists and political leaders began to ask another question: Would it be possible to use the power of the atom to create a bomb, one whose power would be so great that it would force America's enemies to surrender?

In 1943 American scientists set to work to see if they could answer that question. Strangely, they did not look for the answer in shiny modern laboratories. They were working in small shacks near a town called Los Alamos in the deserts of New Mexico. Here, under the leadership of a brilliant physicist named J. Robert Oppenheimer, a team of researchers began to work on the weapon that would so convincingly end the war.

Their top secret weapons research program was called the "Manhattan Project." Between 1943 and 1945, the committee in Congress that authorized payment for the project provided two billion dollars, an almost unimaginable sum of money in 1945. Few members of Congress even knew of the existence of the Manhattan Project. Fewer still knew of its purpose. Those who did hoped that two billion dollars would provide the key to victory over the Axis powers, that is, Germany and Japan.

The scientists who went to Los Alamos came from all over the country. They were the best minds

Physicist J. Robert Oppenheimer headed the Manhattan Project, the research program that developed the atomic bomb.

available. Many had friends and brothers who had died in battle, so they worked almost feverishly, with a sense of purpose and mission. They knew the theory behind the bomb, but they spent countless hours trying to discover how to apply that theory to actually produce a working weapon.

The surrender of Germany in May 1945 was a relief. At least the United States no longer had to worry about Hitler and the possibility that Nazi Germany was developing an atomic bomb of its own. But the war in the Pacific against Japan seemed as if it would never end. The Japanese were becoming more and more desperate as the war was turning against them. They seemed to be digging in for a long, brutal, hopeless fight to defend their homeland. Battalions of Americans would surely be killed in an invasion of the Japanese mainland. Hard-won American victories during the spring and summer of 1945 only convinced President Truman and his advisers that the Japanese were tough opponents.

Then, on July 16, the scientists at Los Alamos found their answer. The tremendous fireball that rose over the desert told them that they held the key to victory over Japan. Immediately, word was sent to the president.

As commander in chief of the United States armed forces, the president had final authority over the bomb and whether it would actually be used against Japan. Although Truman did not make the decision alone, he is the one we think of when we recall this awesome event. His motives are the most interesting to think about. Who was Harry S. Truman and how did this tremendous responsibility fall to him?

The Rise of Harry Truman

Harry Truman never struck people as the kind of person destined to become president. Unlike most American presidents, he did not start his career as a lawyer, politician, or military hero. Rather, he started out as a "haberdasher"—that is, a men's clothing salesman—in Kansas City. Nevertheless, he became the thirty-third occupant of the White House when Pres. Franklin D. Roosevelt suddenly died on April 12, 1945.

In November 1944, President Roosevelt had won a fourth term of office. No one had ever been elected to the presidency more than twice. But Roosevelt was an inspirational leader who had guided the nation through some difficult times. The first test of his ability to lead was the Great Depression of the 1930s. Then he steered the United States through three years of World War II.

British Prime Minister Winston Churchill worked closely with President Roosevelt in shaping Allied strategy against Germany and Japan.

When he campaigned for office for the fourth time in 1944, he told voters that it would be bad policy for the nation to "change horses in the middle of the stream." The voters apparently thought he was right because they voted for him again, keeping him in office to see the nation through the rest of the war. Many thought that he would choose the influential James Byrnes to be his vice president. Instead, joining him on the ticket was a little-known senator from Missouri by the name of Harry Truman.

The world of the 1940s was a stage filled with the commanding presence of famous and infamous leaders. The stern power of Adolf Hitler led Nazi Germany from visions of world conquest to near ruin. In Japan the people revered Emperor Hirohito as a god, and his soldiers willingly died for him.

Vice President Truman sits next to President Roosevelt during a press conference. Inexperienced and relatively unknown, Truman became the president of the United States after Roosevelt's sudden death.

"To me [the reasons for using the atomic bomb] have always seemed compelling and clear."

Henry Stimson, secretary of war

"The decision seems so baffling."

Walter Isaacson, journalist

England boasted Sir Winston Churchill, the cigar-smoking prime minister who even today is thought of as one of the most inspirational leaders of the twentieth century. The Soviet Union was in the grip of Joseph Stalin. Stalin joined with the United States, France, and England in fighting Hitler, but he was proving to be a troublesome ally. The United States had its own share of heroes—generals like Dwight Eisenhower, George Patton, and Douglas MacArthur. Americans felt confident that Roosevelt belonged on the world stage alongside these giants.

Sadly, Roosevelt never saw the end of the war he had led for so long. Thrust onto the stage in his place was that unknown, untested vice president. Momentous events were already in motion, and America wondered what Truman would do. How would he bring the war to a close? How would he deal with the Germans and the Japanese after the war? Would he be able to stand up to Stalin and the Soviet Union? Was he strong and forceful enough as a leader to keep the United States from being taken advantage of in the negotiations and treaties connected with the end of the war?

These are the kinds of questions that Truman himself must have pondered throughout the spring and summer of 1945.

A Terrible Secret

Two weeks after Roosevelt died, on April 24, Truman received a brief, mysterious letter from Secretary Stimson. In his letter, Stimson referred to a "highly secret matter" he thought Truman needed to know about as soon as possible. The following day, April 25, the men met in Truman's office. With them was General Groves, the military director of the Manhattan Project. During this meeting, Truman learned for the first time the awful truth about the purpose of the Manhattan Project—that soon, the United States would have a weapon of unimaginable power. From this date on, an important question would dominate the new president's thoughts: Should the United States use the atomic bomb against its enemies?

Not until the evening of July 16 did Truman really have to face the need to make a decision, for until this date the bomb existed only on paper. Truman was in Potsdam, preparing for his conference with Churchill and Stalin. He knew that that morning the scientists in New Mexico would conduct their first test to see if the bomb would really work. That evening he was told in a top secret coded cable that the efforts of the Los Alamos scientists had finally paid off. In what was called the "Trinity" test, they exploded the world's first atomic weapon in the New Mexico desert.

In the days that followed, Truman made his decision. On July 24, 1945, he gave the order that would change the course of history. On August 6, that order was carried out over the Japanese city of Hiroshima. Whatever his other accomplishments may have been, Truman will be remembered as the only American president ever to order the wartime use of atomic bombs.

Scientists prepare an atomic bomb for experimental detonation.

0.034 SEC.
N
100 METERS

The world's first atomic bomb is exploded during the "Trinity" test in the New Mexico desert. Even the developers of the bomb were startled by the display of such awesome power.

A chalkboard bears the long-awaited message that the war is over. Many Americans believed that the bombing of Japan marked the end of American bloodshed.

Americans responded to the bombing of Japan with relief and jubilation because it seemed to bring about the Japanese surrender on August 14. Just like that, the long war was over! In cities across the United States, people poured into the streets in spontaneous celebrations. For days life was like a carnival. Finally no more stars would have to be placed in the windows of American homes—stars that said that in this house lives the family of a fallen soldier. No longer would wives, fathers, and mothers have to hear those cruel words, " . . . killed in action . . . highest bravery . . . our nation's deepest regrets." Once again freedom and democracy had w₵ Dictators who wanted to take that freedom away were defeated. America savored its moment of triumph before beginning the long task of picking up the pieces left behind by the war.

Picking Up the Pieces

After so many years of sacrifice Americans were eager to get life back to normal. Soldiers came home to parades and confetti. They married and started raising families. Many were able to continue their education because the government was paying for college under the "G.I. Bill." The factories that had turned out planes and tanks now started turning out refrigerators and cars, and anyone who wanted a job could have one. The United States was able to deal with its former enemies as friends, making them important allies, even giving them millions of dollars to rebuild their cities. As a nation, the United States felt comfortable in its new role as the most powerful country in history. Because of the bomb, the United States would be able to defend freedom anywhere it had to. The nation was proud in victory, prosperous in peace.

And so, World War II passed into the history books.

But underneath it all, people began to think more about what *really* happened in the sky over Hiroshima that morning of August 6, 1945. The more people thought about it, the less clear and simple that decisive end to World War II became. What started to bother people was that the United States did not win the war for any of the usual reasons. There was no major battle. American troops were not necessarily tougher, more resolved, or more heroic. They did not win because they could shoot straighter, or even just because there were more of them.

In the end, the United States brought the war in the Pacific to a close with the help of a strange force that few could fully understand. Japan and

A young Japanese man suffers from burn wounds. Why were the bombs dropped on civilians rather than military bases?

Germany had undergone massive bombing, as had England. But no single weapon, dropped from a single plane, had been able to devastate an entire city, to engulf that city in a ball of fire whose temperature was one million degrees, to kill tens of thousands of people in seconds, to spread a mysterious radioactivity that claimed lives years after the smoldering rubble had been carted away. Such a weapon was like something from another world, something so horrible and destructive that no one could ever hide from it. It was a weapon that had a kind of life of its own. It was a weapon that symbolized science gone insane. It was a weapon that kept people awake at night.

Was the Bomb Necessary?

What before seemed clear and simple now seemed murky. Historians started to ask questions that only a few had dared ask in that summer of 1945. Just why *did* the United States drop the atomic bomb on Japan? Was the bombing of Hiroshima necessary? Was Japan about to surrender anyway? If not, could the United States have ended the war in a less savage way? If the clock could be turned back, would U.S. leaders make the same decision?

These questions gave rise to others. How did President Truman really feel about his decision? What role did the military play in the decision-making process? Were there people in Truman's administration who opposed the use of the bomb?

The questions kept coming. Why did the United States drop the bomb on cities rather than military bases? After the first bomb, did the second one have to be used as well? What would have happened if the first bomb had been dropped off shore or in a secluded area? Would such a demonstration of its fearsome power have persuaded the Japanese to give up?

"Did we have to drop the Bomb? You bet your life we did."

Harold M. Agnew, former director, Los Alamos Scientific Laboratory

"Should the Bomb have been used against Japan? There's no simple answer."

Richard M. Nixon, president of the U.S., 1969-1974

And then there was the most intriguing question of all: Did the president have other, secret reasons for ordering this terrible weapon to be used?

We may never know the answer to some of these questions. Time is the historian's enemy. With every passing year, historians have to dig deeper to find the answers to questions like these. Memories grow dim, the people who were there die. But time can be an ally, too. It allows facts and evidence to come to the surface. It gives historians a chance to think about what the facts and evidence mean. Most importantly, it provides a chance to ask the right questions.

Time has teased us with questions about Hiroshima. Let's look at the answers time has yielded.

Two

Did Truman Drop the Atomic Bomb to Save Lives?

(opposite page) American soldiers stand over a dead Japanese soldier. Most military officials believed that Truman saved American troops by bringing the war to a hasty end.

The world naturally looks back on the atomic bombing of Hiroshima to decide if America's leaders acted wisely. Historians, military planners, generals, and presidents want to learn whatever they can about how Truman made his decision to go ahead with the use of the atomic bomb. One question they have repeatedly asked is this: What would have happened if the United States had not used the bomb but instead had tried to end the war by a massive invasion of Japan? In fact, plans were made for just such a possibility.

For months prior to the bombing, American commanders had been working on two important plans for an invasion of Japan. If Truman had chosen this option, the first phase, called *Olympic*, would have taken place on November 1, 1945. American forces would have launched an assault on the southern Japanese island of Kyushu. The commanders thought American forces could easily have established a foothold in Japan here. Even though Kyushu is an important part of Japan, it is six hundred miles away from Tokyo, the capital city, so the island would have been hard for Japanese armed forces to defend. If necessary, a second operation, called *Coronet*, would have taken place in March

A map of Japan shows its proximity to China and the Soviet Union. In 1904-1905, Japan won great power status when it defeated the Russians in the Russo-Japanese War. In 1937, Japan seized the coastal cities and military bases of China. During World War II, Allies tried to stem Japan's aggressive, expansionist policies.

> "I wanted to save a half million boys on our side. . . . I never lost any sleep over my decision."
>
> Pres. Harry S. Truman

> "The myth of 500,000 lives saved . . . helped deter Americans from asking troubling questions about the use of the atomic bombs."
>
> Barton J. Bernstein, professor of history, Stanford University

1946. Coronet's objective was control of the plains surrounding Tokyo and, finally, control of the capital city itself.

Of course, American troops never had to carry out either of these operations. The Japanese surrendered after the atomic bombs destroyed Hiroshima and Nagasaki, bringing the war to an abrupt and dramatic end. Yet the question remains whether invasion would have been a better solution.

In the years following the war, President Truman expressed his belief that invading Japan would have been a mistake. He claimed that as many as a half-million American lives would have been lost in such an invasion; put differently, a half-million American lives were saved by his decision to drop the atomic bombs. And Truman was not the only leader who made such a claim. General Groves estimated that close to a million Americans would have died. Prime Minister Churchill put his estimate at over a million.

As the years following the war went by, the belief that using the bomb had actually *saved* more lives than it took came to be thought of by many as a fact. It is easy to understand why people accepted Truman's claim. The United States is the only country that has ever used atomic weapons in war, so Americans needed to believe that Truman's decision was right. They needed to believe that that decision was made strictly because of the needs of

American fleets went up in smoke after the Japanese bombed a sleeping Pearl Harbor on December 7, 1941.

war and not for less noble reasons.

An American marine fighting in the South Pacific in 1944 and 1945 might have found Truman's claim easy to accept. He would have seen firsthand the results of Japanese resistance.

The Price of Victory

After destroying the American fleet at Pearl Harbor in December 1941, Japan quickly gained control of most of the Pacific, which meant control of the many islands that became important naval bases and airstrips. The American navy and marines acquired the job of regaining control over those islands. As the United States rebuilt its fleet, American troops, in a series of fierce island battles, pushed the Japanese westward toward their homeland.

But the price they paid for these victories was terrible. The Japanese were tough opponents, and they gave up control of those islands only inches at

Rows of graves bear tribute to the great number of soldiers who died during World War II.

A Japanese tank prepares to fire on marine forces at Okinawa. Almost fifty thousand Americans were wounded or killed on this island.

a time. The vicious fighting that took place as American troops hopped from island to island cost thousands of lives. The battle for Iwo Jima, for example, took place in February and March 1945. In taking this eight-square-mile dot of land, over twenty-five thousand Americans were killed or wounded, and almost every one of the island's twenty-one thousand Japanese troops fought to the death.

Iwo Jima was just a warm-up. Between mid-April and mid-June, American and Japanese troops met on the island of Okinawa. In one of the bloodiest battles of the war, almost fifty thousand Americans were killed or wounded. Seventy thousand Japanese soldiers were killed, along with an estimated eighty thousand Okinawan civilians.

American troops knew that every battle they fought cost thousands of lives. In an invasion of Japan, the fighting would only have been more savage, and the number of lives lost on both sides would have been tragic. Later, Americans learned

Harry Truman calculates casualty rates during a meeting with advisers. Did Truman really believe that a half-million Americans would have died had he not decided to drop the bomb?

that Japan had gathered two million reserve troops, and that as many as thirty million civilians were armed (some with bamboo spears) and prepared for a long fight. Most Japanese would have died for their emperor rather than suffer the dishonor of surrender. American forces would have faced desperate resistance.

Thus, to American marines sitting on ships waiting for the start of an invasion of Japan, the atomic bomb may have come as a kind of blessing. They knew that although many lives were lost in the destruction of Hiroshima and Nagasaki, more lives had been lost in some of the "conventional" battles—that is, battles fought with troops, planes, tanks, and ships—in the Pacific. The marines who had fought in such battles would have easily believed President Truman when he said that he dropped the bomb to save American lives.

The Cost of an Invasion of Japan

Casualties are a fact of war. Although money is spent on weapons and supplies, the real "cost" of any military operation is the number of people killed or wounded. Wartime leaders plan military operations that will achieve their goal at the lowest possible cost in lives. When Truman claimed that his decision to drop the bomb saved a half-million American lives, he seemed to be suggesting that he had no real choice: To end the war, the United States could either invade Japan at a very high cost in human life—or use the bomb.

There is one catch, though. Some records suggest that Truman may not have really believed that a half-million Americans would have died in an invasion. Or that if he did believe that figure, he did so only because he wanted to believe it in order to live with the horrifying results of his decision to drop the bomb. Is it true that he did not believe this estimate? No one knows for sure. But if he did not,

Virtually unknown before his vice presidency, Harry Truman made the controversial decision to use the atomic bomb to end the war with Japan. Would Japan have surrendered had the atomic bomb not been dropped?

then some intriguing questions remain. What did Truman believe about the cost of an invasion of Japan? Would Olympic and Coronet have succeeded? At what cost? Did the United States have other means of ending the war? Could other strategies have worked?

A puzzle to historians is that the numbers President Truman used when he talked or wrote about the cost of an invasion kept changing. During the years that he was still in office, Truman usually put the number at 250,000. Sometimes, he used a lower figure, 200,000. These would have been heavy losses—but far less heavy than a half-million.

After he left the White House early in 1953,

"To quell the Japanese resistance man by man and conquer the country yard by yard might well require the loss of a million American lives and half that number of British."

Winston Churchill, prime minister of Britain during the war years

"This invasion of the Tokyo Plain should be relatively inexpensive."

Joint Staff Planners

"It was a question of saving hundreds of thousands of American lives."

Pres. Harry S. Truman

"I do not anticipate such a high rate of loss."

Gen. Douglas MacArthur, U.S. commander in the Pacific

Truman began to raise the estimate. In the first draft of his autobiography, he put the number at 300,000. But when the autobiography was actually published in 1955, he had changed the number to 500,000. And there were public occasions after that when he raised the estimate all the way to a million!

Of course, to say for sure how many people would have died in a battle that was never fought is impossible. Nevertheless, the differences in the numbers Truman stated were large ones. Where did he get the information on which he based these estimates? And why did the numbers change?

War Plans

The record shows that Truman was given official government estimates *before* the bombing of Hiroshima. These casualty figures were much lower than even Truman's early conservative figure of 200,000. They came from several different sources. The first estimate came from the Joint Chiefs of Staff, the high-level representatives from each of the armed services who advise the president about military affairs. The Joint Chiefs of Staff appointed a special group called the Joint War Plans Committee. The job of this committee was to make recommendations to the president about war plans and operations in the Pacific.

The Joint War Plans Committee studied a number of different plans for invading Japan, and on June 15, 1945, turned in its report. The committee concluded that about forty-six thousand Americans would probably be killed in an invasion of Japan. Further, they believed that Coronet—the 1946 invasion of the area around Tokyo—would probably not even be necessary because Japan would have already surrendered by that time. In that case, a total of perhaps twenty-five thousand would be lost, all of them in the assault on Kyushu.

Another authority who advised President Truman

Gen. George C. Marshall formulated the Marshall Plan, an economic program to aid war-ravaged Europe.

during the spring and summer before the bombing of Hiroshima was Gen. George C. Marshall. He was the respected military figure and statesman who conceived the plan to contribute money to rebuild Europe after the war. By turning America's war-torn allies and former enemies into productive and prosperous nations, the so-called "Marshall Plan" was a major foreign policy success for the United States.

Other Casualty Estimates

During the 1950s, Truman claimed that he got the half-million figure from conversations he had with Marshall. But records that were made of a meeting between Truman and Marshall on June 18, 1945—almost three weeks before the Hiroshima bombing—show that Marshall did not use that fig-

Gen. Douglas MacArthur commanded Pacific operations during the war. MacArthur estimated that the U.S. saved 100,000 American lives by using the bomb to end the war.

ure. During that meeting, he told Truman that during the first thirty days of an invasion of Kyushu, when most of the losses would probably be suffered, the United States could expect to lose about thirty-one thousand soldiers.

Other evidence supports the belief that Marshall would not have given the president an estimate as high as 500,000. As army chief of staff, Marshall was a member of the Joint Chiefs of Staff, so he saw the report of the Joint War Plans Committee. In a memo to Secretary Stimson, Marshall said that he had read the committee's June 15 report—and that he agreed with its findings!

In addition, on June 18, Marshall received a cable from Gen. Douglas MacArthur, the U.S. commander of Pacific operations. While the Joint War Plans Committee was doing its work, MacArthur and his staff were making their own on-the-scene estimate. The number that MacArthur arrived at was higher—about 100,000—but it was not anywhere near a half-million.

With these official estimates in hand, how likely is it, then, that Marshall would have advised Truman at any time that the cost of an American invasion of Japan would have been as high as 500,000? If he did give the president that figure, perhaps in a private conversation, why did Truman state a figure so much higher than what his own sources told him? Did Marshall have other information that has not come to light?

Figures from the Joint Staff Planners

The Joint War Plans Committee and General Marshall were not Truman's only sources of information. The Joint Staff Planners, another group of military advisers, reported their views to the president on July 9, 1945. Their report came almost a month before the United States dropped the atomic bomb on Hiroshima and two weeks before

Truman's July 24 order to strike. The Joint Staff Planners placed their emphasis on the possible outcome of Operation Coronet in March 1946. In their view, this phase of the invasion would probably not have been very costly. They based their view on the geography of the Tokyo area. Overall, Japan is a mountainous country. The mountain terrain would normally make an invasion difficult. American forces would have had difficulty finding places to land, and the few places available could have been heavily fortified. The terrain around Tokyo, however, is comparatively flat. American assault troops would have been able to land at many different places at the same time. They would have been able to maneuver quickly and move supplies and equipment easily. These advantages would have made it difficult, if not impossible, for Japanese troops—already tied up in defending Kyushu—to mass around Tokyo and concentrate at any point where they could have repelled an American assault.

Marine amphibious forces land at Okinawa. Here, marines position themselves on the beach as supporting troops wade ashore. Almost fifty thousand Americans were killed or wounded at Okinawa.

"If we had invaded the main islands, it would have cost perhaps a million American casualties, certainly more than a million Japanese."

Richard M. Nixon, president of the U.S., 1969-1974

"Actually, there is no evidence that any top military planner or major American policy maker ever believed that an invasion would cost that many lives."

Barton J. Bernstein, professor of history, Stanford University

Several other key military officers, often writing privately, have expressed their views about the planned invasion. Nearly all of them agree that an invasion of Japan could probably have been carried out without the huge loss of life that Truman, Churchill, and others feared.

In fact, not a single official estimate from that summer supports Truman's claim that a half-million lives was the price to be paid for ending the war without using the atomic bomb.

The government archives in Washington, D.C., contain reports, memos, letters, cables, and minutes of meetings. These papers form one kind of picture of events during the weeks and months that led up to the bombing of Hiroshima. Each page adds to what is known about the war.

But the archives do not preserve the unofficial meetings, the unplanned conversations, the phone calls, and the quick notes that were thrown away. It is not difficult to imagine that in exchanges like these information was traded, opinions were given, and decisions were made for reasons that cannot be clearly explained decades later. If by some magic a historian could get at some of these sources of information, then some of the differences between Truman's views and the views of others might be more easily explained.

Motives for Misleading Estimates

Examination of possible motives of people involved in the moment-to-moment decision making can lead to possible explanations. Consider the commanders of the armed forces, who would normally be any president's most important source of information and counsel about military strategy. How might their motives affect the information they gave to the president? It is easy to imagine that they would take an optimistic view of how a conventional land and sea assault would go. They would

therefore give low estimates of the cost of battle. Why? They had fought the bulk of the war. Their troops had suffered the losses during years of major battles in the Pacific. Then, just at the moment when they would be poised to deliver the knockout punch, a device like the bomb would make them almost useless. They would want to have a hand in carrying out a historic military mission. They would want to finish the job they had started. A low estimate of the cost of an invasion might make it more likely that invasion plans would be approved and that the invasion itself would take place. They and their troops would keep their role as America's guardians.

Victims wait to receive first aid in the demolished city of Hiroshima. Could the U.S. have used another strategy to end the war?

What about President Truman's motives? It seems clear that in the years following the war, he needed to convince Americans—and the world—that his decision to drop the bomb was the right one. This need became greater as more and more people in the 1950s condemned the bombing and argued that atomic weapons were immoral and should be banned from America's arsenal. The horrifying picture of the mushroom cloud rising over Hiroshima and photographs taken at the site in the days that followed etch their way into the memory of anyone who has seen them. Some people condemned Truman for his decision to use the bomb. Thus, it makes sense that he would want to give a high estimate of the cost of a conventional land and sea assault. He would want to

An American pilot prepares for takeoff to Japan. Many pilots were shot down over the Pacific, prompting Truman to end the use of conventional warfare.

make it appear that his decision was the only reasonable one that could have been made. To the many Americans who were becoming uneasy about the bomb's use, Truman's words of assurance must have been comforting.

Were either of these possible motives—the military's desire to retain its role as guardian of America and Truman's desire to safeguard his reputation—strong enough to lead them to falsify projected death figures? Or at least to ignore evidence that would have led them to a different figure? We can only guess the answer to these questions—or we can seek other possible explanations for the decision to use the bomb. Could the decision have been the result of diplomatic failures, that is, of botched attempts on the part of American officials to help Japan find a way to surrender with honor?

Three

Did Truman Drop the Bomb Because of Diplomatic Errors?

(opposite page) An aerial view of Tinian Island, the base from which U.S. forces dropped atomic bombs on Hiroshima and Nagasaki.

Like a boxer during the late rounds of a difficult match, Japan was reeling during the spring and summer of 1945. In spite of the stiff resistance that American forces met with in places like Iwo Jima and Okinawa, Japan was defeated. By the summer of 1945, most of its navy had been sunk. Its air force could do little more than carry out kamikaze attacks—suicide missions in which a pilot would deliberately fly his bomb-filled plane into an American ship. Its industry was destroyed, its airfields were useless, its harbors were mined. Food was in short supply, and there was no fuel to power the equipment and weapons that remained. American B-29 bombers attacked Japanese cities repeatedly with only small losses on the American side. In contrast, Japanese losses were high. For example, on the night of May 10, 1945, bombing raids on Tokyo left an estimated 124,000 dead—more than later died at either Hiroshima or Nagasaki. Making matters more desperate for Japan was the end of the war in Europe. The United States would now be able to direct all of its military might against Japan. A Japanese defeat seemed unavoidable.

Many of President Truman's advisers, including Gen. Dwight Eisenhower, told him that it was only

51861 AC

Air Force Chief of Staff Henry "Hap" Arnold believed that Japan would have surrendered even if the atomic bomb had not been dropped.

a matter of time before Japan would surrender. Air Force Chief of Staff Henry "Hap" Arnold was more specific. He stated that the Japanese would surrender by September or October, even without an invasion. After the war, these views were confirmed in the U.S. Strategic Bombing Survey's report. This report discussed in detail the results of American military operations in the Pacific. It concluded that "certainly prior to 31 December 1945 and in all probability prior to 1 November 1945 Japan would have surrendered, even if the atomic bombs had not been dropped." If Truman's military advisers were right, then the atomic bombing of Japan may have been unnecessary because the war would have ended soon anyway.

The Japanese View

In the decades since 1945, historians have asked many questions about what was happening in the Japanese Imperial Palace, the seat of government in Tokyo, during the final months of the war. Did Japanese officials believe that their country was defeated? Were they actually looking for a way to surrender with honor to the Americans, or did they intend to continue the war for as long as possible? What kinds of political conflicts within the Japanese government were standing in the way of a surrender?

These are important questions. They go directly to the heart of questions related to Truman's decision to drop the bombs. Could the United States have ended the war in the Pacific by diplomatic rather than military means? Might Truman have missed a chance to negotiate a surrender that Japan would have accepted? Was Japan ready to surrender before the United States dropped the bombs?

If so, then why did Truman order that the bombs be dropped?

It is difficult to reconstruct the sequence of

General Tojo ordered the surprise bombing of Pearl Harbor on December 7, 1941. To many people, this attack proved that Japan could not be trusted.

events that led to the failure of the United States and Japan to find a diplomatic settlement of the war in the Pacific. Evidence about Japanese intentions during this period is incomplete. But the United States knew much of what was happening in Japan's inner political circles from a series of intercepted cables and messages. Earlier in the war, U.S. intelligence—the arm of the military whose task was to gather information about the enemy's war operations—had broken Japan's secret military and diplomatic codes. Diaries kept by President Truman

Emperor Hirohito enjoyed a god-like status in the eyes of Japanese soldiers, who willingly sacrificed their lives so that he could remain on the throne.

show that he read the intercepted messages. As the spring and summer of 1945 advanced and the Japanese military grew steadily weaker and more demoralized, the theme of these messages became clear: Japan was ready to surrender, and was in fact making frequent diplomatic attempts to negotiate a peace settlement. These messages, combined with the testimony of Japanese officials and military leaders after the war, suggest that the United States might have been able to end the war without an invasion and without dropping the atomic bomb. Nevertheless, the United States continued to make plans for both.

Truman's failure to more actively pursue a negotiated settlement can be defended on the grounds that Japanese officials were not of one mind about the purpose of the war and the value of continuing it. By early 1945 several factions, or special interest groups, had developed in both the Japanese government and the military. These factions disputed among themselves, some trying to find a way to end the war, others arguing that the war should be continued. The resulting confusion made it difficult for Truman and his advisers to decide on the best course of action.

Japanese Factions

The factions who supported the war and wanted to carry on with it were made up largely of army generals. The "militarists," as they have often been called, wanted to continue the war because they believed that Japan could still win. They believed, in spite of recent Japanese defeats, that Japan's destiny was to be the dominant power in Asia and in the Pacific. They believed that if they did not extend their empire in these regions they would be dominated by larger powers such as China, Russia, and the United States. They were so committed to the war that even after the atomic bombs were dropped they wanted to carry on with the fight. In the meantime, they hoped that the Soviet Union would enter the war in the Pacific on Japan's side. This hope had two sources. First, earlier in the war, Japan and the Soviets had signed a "non-aggression pact"—a treaty agreeing not to oppose one another militarily. Second, the Soviets and the United States had been allies in the war against Hitler in Europe. But now they seemed to be at odds with each other over the

"I believed the atomic bomb would be successful and would force the Japanese to accept surrender on our terms."

James Byrnes, President Truman's secretary of state

"[The atomic bomb] had nothing to do with the end of the war."

Gen. Curtis LeMay

During the war, Japanese officials used coded messages from the "Purple" machine to communicate with one another. An official could type a message on the keyboard and it would print out in an extremely complex code known only to the Japanese.

future of postwar Europe. The militarists in Japan were thus counting heavily on Soviet support in the war against the United States.

Other factions in Japan, however, were exploring ways to end the war. Early in 1945, for example, the *jushin,* or "important subjects"—a council made up of former Japanese leaders—conferred with Emperor Hirohito, urging him to find a way to end the war. The *jushin* and other moderate factions believed that the Soviets would never enter the war as allies of Japan. They did, however, hope that the Soviets might at least remain neutral and, acting as a kind of go-between with the United States, help Japan negotiate more favorable surrender terms. Representatives of these factions approached the embassies of other countries, including Sweden, Switzerland, and Portugal, with the same purpose. In spite of their fear of the army generals, the moderates found ways to involve embassies around the world in the attempt to find an honorable way out of the war.

A New Japanese Government

Japanese peace efforts intensified in April 1945. America invaded Okinawa, and Stalin set aside the non-aggression pact. These events prompted a crisis leading to the formation of a new government. At its head was retired Adm. Kantaro Suzuki, a moderate who wanted the war to end and who was offered the position primarily because of the influence of the *jushin.* He appointed as foreign minister Shigenori Togo, a former ambassador to the Soviet Union. He was also opposed to the war. Togo took the position on the condition that he could approach the Soviets to see if they would persuade the United States to offer surrender terms more favorable to Japan. If the Soviets would help, Suzuki and Togo were prepared to give up to them territories in northeast China that Japan had captured earlier in

"Certainly . . . Japan would have surrendered, even if the atomic bombs had not been dropped."

The United States Strategic Bombing Survey, July 1, 1946

"It was not one atomic bomb, or two, which brought surrender; it was the experience of what an atomic bomb will actually do to a community, *plus the dread of many more*, that was effective."

Arthur Compton, physicist

Kantaro Suzuki, retired Japanese admiral, was opposed to the war. In April 1945, Suzuki was appointed head of a new Japanese government, at which time he appointed other moderates who wanted the war to end.

the war. Eventually, in late June, Togo would get his wish to approach the Soviets, but Stalin's replies to his pleas were evasive. Togo did not know that Stalin had already decided to enter the war against Japan sometime during the summer.

By the summer of 1945, then, influential forces in the Japanese government clearly wanted to end the war. Moderates who opposed the war had gained a majority in the Japanese parliament.

Diplomats throughout the world were searching for a way to establish lines of communication between Japan and the United States. One intercepted cable shows that Hirohito had taken the advice of the *jushin* and become actively involved in the debate over peace and war. This was an important sign, for the Japanese emperor by tradition stays aloof from politics.

Why, then, were the two nations unable to come to terms of surrender both could accept?

The Difficult Idea of Surrender

Americans generally believe that the war did not end sooner because Japan simply refused to surrender. Yet a major stumbling block to surrender in Japan, according to historian Robert C. Butow and others, was that the United States insisted on an unconditional surrender. To most Japanese, an unconditional surrender—one that would have allowed the United States to dictate *all* of its terms—was not acceptable. To a proud nation, built on a code of

Japanese kamikaze pilots wait for flight instructions. Inspired by the code of self-sacrifice and patriotism, this force of suicide pilots inflicted heavy damage at Okinawa.

loyalty, bravery, self-sacrifice, and honor in combat, surrender on any terms was humiliating. It meant that Japanese culture, history, and traditions would have been trampled on by American invaders. Further, the war against the United States had almost a religious quality. The soldier was fighting for the glory of his country. But more important, he was fighting for his emperor, who in his eyes was a kind of god. For years, in fact, kamikaze pilots whose missions were cancelled by the end of the war felt disgraced that they had been unable to die for their emperor. Thus a vital question for the Japanese was whether the emperor could remain on the throne. They feared not only that he would be deposed, but also that he could be tried by the United States as a war criminal, and even executed.

A Political Question

In these circumstances, surrender became a political question in Japan. The factions in the government and military that opposed surrender on any terms remained just powerful enough to block the efforts of the moderates. This paralyzed the government. It was even widely feared that some military units would have openly defied any order to lay down their arms. Fear of the military leaders among the moderate factions was so widespread that even Premier Suzuki felt obligated to pretend that he was pursuing the war to a victorious end. In June, for example, he issued a statement that the loss of Okinawa "improved Japan's strategic position"—that it was part of a strategy designed to lure American forces closer to the Japanese mainland where they could be trapped and gloriously defeated! Further, the government made additional efforts to sustain the war effort: "peace agitators" were threatened; production of war materials was increased; people were urged to stockpile food. In this climate of conflicting views, the United States made repeated de-

Presidential adviser Joseph Grew thought that the Japanese would surrender if they were assured that Emperor Hirohito would not be deposed. Why did Truman refuse to make this concession?

"[The intercepted cables were] real evidence of a Japanese desire to get out of the war."

James V. Forrestal, President Truman's secretary of the navy

"Japan's peace feelers ranged between vague and arrogant, and they never approached American expectations."

Barton J. Bernstein, history professor, Stanford University

mands for an unconditional surrender—and the Japanese repeatedly rejected them.

American leaders knew of Japan's concern about the emperor. Yet for reasons that may never be clear, they failed to respond to that concern. Some presidential advisers, including Secretary Stimson and Undersecretary of State Joseph Grew, urged the president to assure the Japanese that Hirohito could remain on the throne. Grew, in fact, met with the president and begged him to make a statement to that effect. Truman's diaries suggest that he had no objection to this change in American surrender terms. If this assurance would have strengthened the position of the peace party in Japan, why did Truman never offer it?

Why Unconditional Surrender?

One possible explanation is that the president feared that if he made this one concession, the militarists in Japan would have demanded more concessions. He wanted to avoid taking any action that might encourage the militarists, give them more influence in the decision-making process, and thus end any hopes for a negotiated end to the war. Further, at the time of the president's meeting with Grew, the battle for Okinawa was not going well for American forces. The president's military advisers persuaded him that such a statement would be seen by Japanese militarists as a sign of American weakness.

Another possible explanation for Truman's failure to change the surrender terms is that doing so would have hurt him politically. Resentment against Japan ran deep with many Americans because of the surprise attack on Pearl Harbor. To many Americans, Japan was a warlike nation that had to be crushed. Many newspapers and radio commentators used the slogan "Hirohito must go!" to whip up popular opinion against Japan. Sec. of State James

On August 14, 1945, Japan surrendered. What would have happened if the U.S. had not used the atomic bomb?

Byrnes, a shrewd politician who had great influence with the president, could see that Truman would suffer politically if he accepted Japan's conditions for surrender. Members of Congress also urged the president to continue to demand an unconditional surrender. Truman followed their advice.

The Potsdam Declaration

In late July, the peace effort became more complicated. The success of the first atomic weapons test on July 16 left Truman less patient with the Japanese refusal to surrender. Accordingly, on July 26, he issued a final demand for surrender, threatening Japan with "prompt and utter destruction" otherwise. He issued this warning from Potsdam, where he and Stalin were meeting; for this reason it is called the "Potsdam Declaration." The Soviets did not join the United States in signing the declaration, as Great Britain and China did. This convinced some Japanese officials that the Soviets had no intention of entering the war on the American side. What they did not know was that the United States issued the declaration without notifying or consulting the Soviets.

Japanese kamikaze pilots bow down, expressing their willingness to deliberately crash bomb-bearing planes into American installations.

The Potsdam Declaration appeared to be a further demand for unconditional surrender. It provided for eliminating the influence of the Japanese militarists "for all time." It provided for American occupation of Japan after the war. It insisted on America's right to try "war criminals." And it called for the disarming of Japan. But paragraph seven of the declaration stated, in part, that occupation forces "shall be withdrawn from Japan as soon as . . . there has been established a peacefully inclined and responsible government." This statement was as close as Truman ever came to assuring the Japanese that they could determine their own future—a future that, presumably, could include the emperor.

The results of the Potsdam Declaration illustrate a valuable lesson in the difficulties of international politics. The way a single word is translated from one language to another can be the difference between life and death, between peace and war. For two days Japanese leaders struggled over how to respond to America's demand. Togo knew that any official response to the declaration would have to be a flat refusal. Otherwise, the risk that the army generals would try to take over the government would be high. He wanted to avoid making any statement at all and continue to work behind the scenes to get assurances about the emperor. Unfortunately, Premier Suzuki, in his own effort to appease the generals, issued a statement on July 28, rejecting the terms of the Potsdam Declaration. In his statement was the Japanese word *mokusatsu*. This word can be translated into English in several ways. One meaning is "ignore," "treat with silent contempt," or "take no notice of." But another possible meaning is "withhold comment at this time." This interpretation of the word is much more neutral. It implies not a rejection, but merely the wish to think about American terms at greater length. If this is what the Suzuki government meant, then there was still hope for peace. Unfortunately, U.S. officials chose the first meaning. They saw *mokusatsu* as Japan's final rejection of American peace terms.

How would history be different if a different translator had been given the responsibility of translating the Japanese response, and had phrased it in another way? How would Japanese officials have responded to the Potsdam Declaration if they had known of the deadly order Truman had issued to the United States Air Force on July 24?

Efforts of Japanese Diplomats

On August 2, just four days before the atomic bomb was dropped on Hiroshima, William Donovan met with President Truman. Donovan was head of the Office of Strategic Services (OSS), an American intelligence-gathering agency. He informed the president that Japanese diplomats in Switzerland had contacted him, trying to clarify their government's response to the Potsdam Declaration. These diplomats were aware of the political debate taking place in Japan's ruling circles. They suspected that

Sec. of State James Byrnes urged Truman not to concede to Japan's conditions for surrender.

Premier Suzuki's response to the surrender demand was probably the result of his attempt to forge a compromise between rival groups—that it in fact meant nothing. They indicated to Donovan that a "real response" would follow in just a week. They even stated that radio broadcasts saying that Japan rejected the Potsdam Declaration were propaganda meant to raise the morale of the country. These broadcasts were not to be taken as the official Japanese response. Were these Japanese diplomats just stalling for time? Or were they trying to send a real message—that Japan was on the verge of surrender—to Truman through Donovan?

Donovan's report to Truman raises an important diplomatic mystery. It was one more piece of evidence that Japan no longer had the political will to continue the war. It was one more indication to the president that the end of the war was in sight, that it would not be necessary for American troops to in-

On August 2, William Donovan, head of an American intelligence-gathering agency, reported to Truman that Japan was on the verge of surrender. Why did Truman still believe that the bomb was the best course of action?

vade Japan—and that dropping the atomic bomb would not hasten the war's end by more than a few days, or at most a few weeks. The intercepted cables and messages from Japan had already raised the strong possibility that Japan was ready to surrender. The personal involvement of Emperor Hirohito in the debate over peace and war strengthened this possibility. American military authorities were stating to the president their belief that Japan was about to collapse. Then Donovan's report, just days before the bombing, offered the possibility that Japanese officials were pleading for more time, using behind-the-scenes diplomatic channels to inform the president of efforts to get all factions to agree to surrender terms. Why did the president fail to act on Donovan's report? The record gives no answer to this question.

Suspense Mounts

The people of Hiroshima and Nagasaki went about their business in August 1945. While they worked and ate, slept and laughed, the world's powers waited. The Japanese government waited for the Soviets to decide whether they would help Japan, or at least stay neutral. The United States waited for Japan to surrender unconditionally and for the Soviets to decide on a course of action in the Pacific. Any decisive action by Japan, the Soviet Union, or the United States during these days could perhaps have ended the war before August 6.

And in the meantime, the scientists at Los Alamos went ahead with their work. The technicians on Tinian Island went ahead with plans for their mission. The pilots' strike orders remained posted on the wall, while the "Bomb: Special" was undergoing final checks.

The fuse was lit, and it continued to burn.

Four

Did Truman Carefully Consider the Decision to Drop the Bomb?

(opposite page) The mushroom cloud rises moments after the atomic bomb is dropped on Nagasaki.

In 1947, Henry Stimson wrote an article for *Harper's Magazine* called "The Decision to Use the Atomic Bomb." In it he described the decision-making process that led to the bombing of Hiroshima. As secretary of war under Roosevelt and Truman, he had been intimately involved in the discussions of the possible use of the bomb. He had been urged to write the article by officials who were concerned about the small but growing number of people questioning the use of the bomb.

The key word in the title of Stimson's article is "decision." The word *decision* suggests that the bomb was dropped only after careful consideration. It suggests that Truman and his advisers first studied the military situation. They then weighed and discussed the courses of action open to them. Only then did they decide on the most logical one, the one that would achieve the goal of ending the war at the lowest possible cost.

This was the kind of process Stimson described in his article. He recalled a series of clear, orderly steps in the decision-making process, all leading conclusively to Truman's belief that using the bomb was the best course of action. He emphasized many of the issues discussed in previous chapters of this

Two years after the bombing of Japan, Sec. of War Henry Stimson chronicled the decision-making process that led to the use of the bomb. Stimson's account implied that Truman had less devastating options for ending the war.

book: the large number of Americans killed in recent battles, evidence that the Japanese would desperately defend their homeland, and Japan's apparent refusal to surrender. Additionally, he referred to the work of advisory committees that urged use of the bomb for various reasons. In short, he portrayed decision makers firmly in control of events.

Stimson's article had the desired effect. It was widely read, and for years it was accepted as an accurate summary of the events leading to the bombing of Hiroshima and the compelling reasons for that decision.

But is that how it really happened?

Some historians, including Kai Erikson and Barton J. Bernstein, take a different view. They believe that the bombing of Hiroshima was *not* the result of thoughtful decision making, that there never was a "decision" to use the bomb. They would argue that Stimson's recollections were colored by his desire to put American policies and actions in the best possible light. The reasons for using the bomb may have seemed clear to Stimson, but they were not as clear to others, including the president.

Truman's Position

Of course, no one claims that the bombing was an accident. But the events of the last months of the war were confusing and hurried. Truman became president on April 12. He only learned of the purpose of the Manhattan Project on April 25. The pressure on him to drop the bomb was immense. First, brilliant scientists had worked on the bomb for several years, and its development had cost millions of dollars. Further, Americans had been fighting and dying for almost four years, and Japanese resistance promised to prolong the war—at least in the minds of some—for months. When the bomb proved to be a success, the United States had in its hands a weapon that could quickly end the war. Suddenly, an untested president had to decide whether to use this awesome weapon. Historian Martin Sherwin sums up the president's position this way: "Truman did not inherit the question; he inherited the answer." General Groves was more direct; Truman's decision, he said, was "one of noninterference—basically, a decision not to upset the existing plans."

Is it possible, then, that under the pressure of circumstances like these Truman and his advisers did not make a "decision" to use the bomb, but rather had all along taken for granted that the bomb would be used? Might the decision to drop the

"Certainly, there was no question in my mind, or . . . in the mind of . . . any responsible person, but that we were developing a weapon to be employed against the enemies of the United States."

Gen. Leslie Groves, military commander, the Manhattan Project

"I voiced to [Stimson] my grave misgivings . . . because I thought that our country should avoid shocking world opinion by the use of a weapon whose employment was . . . no longer mandatory as a measure to save American lives."

Gen. Dwight Eisenhower

"At no time, from 1941 to 1945, did I ever hear it suggested by the President, or by any other responsible member of the government, that atomic energy should not be used in the war."

Henry Stimson, President Truman's secretary of war

"The Japanese were ready to surrender and it wasn't necessary to hit them with that awful thing."

Gen. Dwight Eisenhower

atomic bomb been made without discussion, without calm thought, without a search for other courses of action?

Three Major Questions

During the spring and summer of 1945, the president's advisers carried on intense discussions about the atomic bomb. The focus of these discussions, however, was not *whether* the bomb should be used. Rather, the focus was *how* the bomb could be used—and used most effectively. These discussions examined three major questions: 1) whether the bomb should be used against Germany or Japan; 2) whether cities or purely military areas should be targeted; and 3) whether some kind of demonstration of the bomb's destructive effects would persuade Japan's leaders to surrender.

1) Should the Bomb Be Dropped on Germany or Japan? Throughout the war, excitement ran high in the United States over possible wartime uses of atomic energy. Spurring the search for a working atomic weapon was the fear that German scientists were also exploring the use of atomic energy. The Manhattan Project, in fact, was born out of fear of Germany, not Japan. Early in the spring of 1945, as American scientists were getting closer to success, they discussed using the bomb on Germany. The fear was repeatedly expressed, however, that if an atomic bomb was dropped on Germany and failed to explode, the Germans would be able to retrieve it and use it to learn how to build their own bomb.

The German surrender in May solved this problem. The danger that Nazi scientists would win the race to build an atomic bomb was over. No longer did American decision makers have to wrestle with the question of whether to drop the bomb in Europe. But by this time, the belief that the bomb would be used on *someone* had taken on its own momentum.

2) Should the Bomb Be Used on Civilian or Military Targets? After the German surrender, policymakers turned their attention immediately to Japan. If the bomb was to be used, a suitable target would have to be chosen. A special Target Committee had already been assembled on April 27 to tackle this question. The committee, which met in the office of J. Robert Oppenheimer, consisted mostly of Manhattan Project scientists.

The committee examined a number of possible targets. Its select list included five: Kyoto, Hiroshima, Yokohama, Niigata, and—the only real military target on the list—Kokura Arsenal. The committee chose these cities because they were large enough to show the full destructive effects of the bomb and because they had not suffered major damage in earlier bombing raids, making further bombing pointless.

The makeup of the target list shows the contra-

Gen. Leslie Groves consults with Manhattan Project scientist J. Robert Oppenheimer during a meeting to determine a target for the world's first atomic bomb.

The aggressive policies of German dictator Adolf Hitler prompted the U.S. to develop the atomic bomb. After Germany surrendered in May of 1945, U.S. officials turned their full attention to locating a bombing site in Japan.

dictory thinking of American policymakers. Truman had stated that he wanted to use the bomb on a military target. His goal, he claimed, was to use the bomb to further cripple the Japanese military without killing thousands of civilians. He wrote in his diary, "I have told . . . Stimson to use it so that military objectives . . . are the target. . . . The target will be purely a military one." Truman's thinking was thus influenced by the moral argument that killing civilians in warfare is wrong and should be avoided whenever possible.

The president was not alone in this belief. Stimson and other advisers repeatedly expressed the belief that targeting civilians in war was immoral. This belief, however, is inconsistent with the fact that all of the cities on the target list, including Kokura, had large civilian populations. This inconsistency becomes more obvious in Truman's announcement of the bombing of Hiroshima. In his statement to the press, he called the city "an important Japanese Army base." After the war he said that he had been told by advisers that the population of each of the target cities was around 60,000. While this was true of the others on the list, Hiroshima's population was 350,000. Was Truman misled? Or did he feel the need to play down the fact that Hiroshima was mainly a civilian area? This contradiction between Truman's apparent wish to drop the bomb on a military target and the fact that Hiroshima was primarily a civilian target has never been fully resolved.

One of the Target Committee's conclusions, though, may shed some light on why Truman acted

Civilians work in a Japanese factory located in Hiroshima, days before the city was obliterated by the atomic bomb. Was it necessary for Truman to target a civilian population rather than a military base?

Scientist James Conant believed that the most important aspect of the atomic bomb was that it attested to the great military power of the U.S.

in a way that seemed to contradict his beliefs. By 1945 the moral argument against killing civilians was not as strong as it had been in previous years. Many bombing raids had already been made on Japanese and German cities, killing thousands of civilians. Although these people were not in combat, many of them were employed producing the planes and tanks that play such an important role in modern warfare. So targeting civilian populations, and the industries that built war equipment, was already becoming more accepted as a way to wear down an enemy's will to continue fighting.

The Role of the Bomb

The Target Committee, then, put aside the moral question. Instead, it emphasized what it called the "psychological effect" of the bomb. Minutes of the committee's meetings suggest that this effect, rather than military need, was guiding the members' thinking. One excerpt, for example, reads:

> Two aspects of [the potential bombing] are 1) obtaining the greatest psychological effect against Japan and 2) making the initial use sufficiently spectacular for the importance of the weapon to be internationally recognized.

This line of thinking was shared by many scientists, military leaders, and advisers. For instance, James Conant, a prominent scientist who wrote one of the earliest studies of the role of atomic weapons in international affairs, argued that the bomb's use was necessary for two reasons. One was to "shock" the Japanese into surrendering. But the other, more important reason was to show the world what the results of another major war might be. The Nobel Prize-winning physicist Arthur H. Compton put it this way: "If the bomb were not used in the present war, the world would have no adequate warning as to what was to be expected if war should break out again."

Thus, a belief shared by many of Truman's sources of counsel was that the bomb had to be used. The bomb was a way to end the war. It was also a way to send a message to Japan and the rest of the world about America's newly found might, and about the change soon to take place in the way wars could be fought. The president wanted to use the bomb in a way that would claim the fewest civilian lives. But Oppenheimer explained that Hiroshima was the best target because its flat terrain would allow the effects of the bomb to "run out," thereby offering a convincing demonstration of its power. Faced with these conflicting considerations, Truman approved the committee's target list.

3) Should the United States Stage a Demonstration of the Bomb? Many scientists and military advisers asked a third question during the months

Would a vivid demonstration of the atomic bomb, such as the one below, have convinced Japanese officials to surrender unconditionally?

40647A.C.

before the bombing of Hiroshima. Would it be possible for the United States to show the power of the bomb in some way other than combat? That is, could the bomb be used as a threat? One suggestion, for example, was to drop the bomb on a Japanese city, but only after giving Japan time to evacuate it. In this way, the bomb's destructive power could be convincingly shown without the need to kill civilians. The main objection to this idea was that Japanese authorities might move large numbers of American prisoners of war into the target city.

A second idea was to strike a purely military target, for instance, a large army base, airfield, or naval harbor. Again, the Target Committee rejected this idea, looking instead for larger targets where the effects of the bomb would be more dramatically displayed.

A third proposal was to stage a demonstration of the bomb. World leaders could be gathered to witness an explosion over, say, a desert or an island. They would then be able to testify to the bomb's awesome power. The objection to this course of action was that the United States would be embarrassed if the bomb was a dud. A failed demonstration would also encourage Japanese militarists to scoff at American surrender demands and to continue the war.

Finally, scientists such as Edward Teller suggested a warning shot over Japan itself. The bomb could be detonated high in the air far out over Tokyo Bay, for example, or over a forest, creating a tremendous firestorm. Many felt that such a vivid display of the bomb would persuade Japan to surrender.

How Seriously Were Alternatives Considered?

Were these ideas ever seriously considered? Did policymakers exert a sincere effort to find a way *not* to use the bomb, or at least not to use it on a largely civilian population? Perhaps they did. But

Like James Conant, physicist Arthur H. Compton argued that the use of the bomb warned other nations of the devastating potential of another major war.

the official record does not show evidence of significant debate.

A case in point is the work of a group called the "Interim Committee." Formed on Secretary Stimson's recommendation after his April 25 meeting with the president, the committee included Stimson, General Marshall, James Byrnes, who would soon become secretary of state, and other top scientific, government, and military figures. As a "blue ribbon" panel of major advisers and policymakers, the Interim Committee had an important voice in questions about the use of the bomb.

A Different Story

The committee met through May and into June to discuss the use of the new bomb and to make recommendations to the president. Stimson said in the *Harper's* article that on May 31 the members "carefully considered" a warning shot or a demonstration. But the minutes of the committee's meeting on that date tell a different story—that the issue of a demonstration was only briefly discussed, and that was over lunch. Members of the committee, such as Arthur H. Compton, have confirmed this. The contradiction between Stimson's recollection and the minutes makes unclear just how quickly the committee rejected the idea. What is clear is that the committee repeated the view of the Target Committee: "We could not give the Japanese any warning; . . . we should seek to make a psychological impression on as many inhabitants as possible. . . . [The] most desirable target would be a vital war plant employing a large number of workers and closely surrounded by workers' houses."

In mid-June some of the scientists working on the bomb urged once again that the United States stage a demonstration. Once again the idea was rejected, this time by the Interim Committee's panel of science advisers, including Oppenheimer and

Scientist Edward Teller argued that a warning detonation over Japan would induce an unconditional surrender. Other scientists disagreed.

"A demonstration of [the atomic bomb] would prove to the Japanese that we could destroy any of their cities at will."

Adm. Lewis Strauss, later chairman of the Atomic Energy Commission

"We did not think exploding one of those things as a firecracker over the desert was likely to be very impressive."

J. Robert Oppenheimer, director, the Manhattan Project

Compton. The panel's conclusion? "We can propose no technical demonstration likely to bring an end to the war; we see no acceptable alternative to direct military use." This appears to have been the last time the possibility was raised.

Some of the evidence, then, leads to this interpretation of events: American officials, including President Truman, made assumptions about the bomb and its military use, and those shared assumptions were never seriously examined. The bombings were the end of a process that had started years be-

Truman decorates Gen. Dwight Eisenhower after the war. Eisenhower, who later became president, opposed the use of the bomb.

fore, a process that was never questioned by the president or anyone else. Under this interpretation of events, Truman's "decision" to drop the atomic bomb was not really a decision at all. Rather, it was a *reaction* to events over which he exerted no real control.

High-Level Opposition

Later investigations, however, show that this interpretation may be misleading, if not false. Recently discovered diaries, memos, and reports written by people involved in the decision-making process suggest that at least a few of Truman's advisers challenged the use of the bomb. Prominent opponents of the bombing included General Eisenhower; Adm. William Leahy, Truman's chief of staff; Richard Bard, who was undersecretary of the navy; John McCloy, the assistant secretary of war; and Joseph Grew, the acting secretary of state. In each case, the opposition of these men was based on their belief that the bomb simply was not needed to bring about a Japanese surrender.

Especially vocal was Eisenhower, the respected military leader who would become president after Truman. As commander of American forces in Europe, Eisenhower was effective both as a general and as a statesman, so his opinion was frequently sought by the White House. Eisenhower met with Secretary Stimson to discuss the upcoming use of the bomb. In a written report responding to that briefing, Eisenhower strongly opposed the use of the bomb. On July 20, he met with the president and urged him not to use the bomb.

Strangely, Eisenhower never revealed that he had this meeting. Gen. Omar Bradley, one of Eisenhower's commanders in Europe, later revealed that the meeting took place. Why did "Ike" keep this discussion to himself? Was he just being a "good soldier," not questioning the decisions of his com-

"The atomic bomb was no 'great decision.'. . . That was not any decision that you had to worry about."

Pres. Harry S. Truman

"[Being involved in the decision to use the atomic bomb was] by far the most searching and important thing that I had to do since I have been here in the office of Secretary of War."

Henry Stimson, President Truman's secretary of war

Gen. Omar Bradley revealed that Eisenhower, in a secret meeting, urged Truman not to use the bomb. Did other discussions take place behind closed doors?

Leo Szilard, a leading opponent of the bomb, circulated a petition to stop atomic warfare.

"The bomb will never be dropped on people. As soon as we get it, we'll use it only to dictate peace."

Ernest O. Lawrence, physicist

"Consideration is to be given to large urban areas of not less than three miles in diameter existing in the larger populated areas."

Target Committee

mander in chief in public? Or had Truman given him convincing reasons for using the bomb? In itself this gap in the record is minor. But it gives later historians an intriguing glimpse behind the closed doors where decisions were being made.

Debates About the Bomb

Another gap in the record leaves historians like Gar Alperovitz wondering about the details of meetings between the president and Admiral Leahy. As Truman's chief of staff and the presiding officer of the Joint Chiefs of Staff, Leahy was an important figure. He met frequently with the president during the summer of 1945 and was with the president in Potsdam. Leahy opposed the use of the bomb, but unfortunately his private papers do not shed very much light on what he said to the president about this issue. Perhaps, like Eisenhower, he felt that he had to carry out the orders of his chief without question.

Opposition to the bomb's use came not just from military figures but from scientific advisers as well. Leo Szilard, one of the scientists who urged development of the bomb before the war, took a leading role in voicing opposition to its use. His efforts were frustrated. Secretary of State Byrnes flatly rejected Szilard's advice, and later, a petition Szilard circulated among scientists who opposed the bomb's use was suppressed. Other opponents included the Committee on the Social and Political Implications of Atomic Energy, otherwise known as the Franck Committee, after its chairman, James Franck. This prominent group of nuclear scientists tried to dispel the view that the atomic bomb would remain America's secret. They argued that its use would increase mistrust between the United States and the Soviets, leading to an arms race and endangering efforts to control atomic energy after the war. The Franck Committee had made the recommendation to the Interim Committee that a demonstration of the bomb be staged. The recommendation was rejected.

If it is true that some of the advisers who spoke with the president, or whose views could have reached the president, argued against dropping the bomb, then the bombing of Hiroshima may not have "just happened." Truman was not, as General Groves characterized him, like "a little boy on a toboggan"—that is, unable to control events that were already in motion. If there was debate, the bombing was more likely the conclusion of a deliberate deci-

Two of the first atomic bombs, "fat man" (top) and "little boy" (bottom).

"It is probable that by intensifying the dread of the new weapon—of which, so far as the Japanese knew, we might have many more—the strike against Nagasaki hastened the surrender."

Herbert Feis, historian

"There is no evidence that [the Nagasaki bombing] speeded the end of the war."

Barton J. Bernstein, historian

sion-making process. Historians know so little about that debate that the solution to this mystery continues to escape them.

The Second Bomb

One more question arises about the decision to drop the bombs. That is, was there really a decision to drop the *second* bomb, which destroyed Nagasaki on August 9? In some senses, the answer is "no." The original strike order from Truman commanded the use of the bomb*s* as soon as *they* were ready. So technicians on Tinian Island worked around the clock to ready the second bomb in response to this order.

Nagasaki was not even on the Target Commit-

The three-storied pagoda of Kiyomizu Temple stands on the edge of a cliff in Kyoto, Japan. Although originally on the list of possible bombing targets, Kyoto was spared to avoid destruction of the many cultural shrines.

tee's original list. It was a substitution for Kyoto. Secretary Stimson, with Truman's agreement, ordered planners to remove Kyoto from the target list. As the former Japanese capital city, Kyoto is the site of a number of cultural shrines. Stimson felt that destruction of these shrines would embitter the Japanese. The United States would then find difficult the development of good postwar relations with Japan.

What is more, Nagasaki was not the original target on the morning of August 9. "Bocks Car," the B-29 that delivered the bomb, was at first headed for Kokura, but bad weather forced the pilot to fly to the backup target, Nagasaki. Even there, cloudy skies

On August 9, 1945, the B-29 "Bocks Car" delivered the bomb that blasted Nagasaki beyond recognition.

The atomic bomb reduced Nagasaki to a field of smoldering rubble. Did Truman have ulterior motives for using a second atomic bomb?

almost ended the mission. But at 11:01, the clouds suddenly broke and the bomb was released. It exploded with the force of twenty-two tons of dynamite. Though more powerful than the Hiroshima bomb, it took fewer lives and did less damage because the bombardier missed the aiming point by over a mile.

Some historians point to two interesting factors that suggest the use of the second bomb was deliberate. One factor is that the bomb that exploded at Hiroshima was very different in its triggering device from the one that exploded at Nagasaki. This difference has led historian Leon Sigal to suggest that Nagasaki was a kind of test firing and that the military wanted to try out two different kinds of bombs. It has even been said that the rush to deliver the second bomb came from a desire to drop it before the Japanese had a chance to surrender. As historian Kai Erikson puts it, "It is hard to slow down, hard to relinquish an advantage, hard to rein the fury. The impulse to charge ahead, to strike at the throat, is so strong a habit of war that it almost ranks as a reflex."

The other factor is that on August 8 the Soviet Union declared war on Japan. The combination of the bombing of Hiroshima on August 6 and Soviet entry into the war on August 8 might very well have convinced Japan that further resistance was futile. Why did Truman not wait to see what the outcome of these events would be?

Did Truman have other reasons for wanting to use the atomic bombs?

Five

Did Truman Drop the Bomb to Impress the Soviets?

Two days before his meeting with Secretary Stimson and General Groves, the new president was about to have his first experience dealing with the Soviet Union. On the schedule was a meeting with the Soviet foreign minister, Vyacheslav M. Molotov. The topic was not Japan or the war in the Pacific, but rather the end of the war in Europe. The date was April 23, 1945.

The meeting was important. It would give both Americans and the Soviets an early answer to at least one question: How tough a negotiator was the new president? How would he deal with the Soviet Union? Would he approach the Soviets in a spirit of cooperation, trying to win them over as Roosevelt had tried to do? Or would he break with Roosevelt's style and confront them?

Truman and Molotov emerged from their meeting. The angry expressions on their faces told observers that the two men were divided. The next day, April 24, Stimson sent his letter to Truman asking for a meeting on the twenty-fifth. Was Stimson thinking about the defeat of Japan? Or was his request a reaction to the stormy meeting between Truman and Molotov?

Throughout the Second World War, the Soviets

had been troublesome allies. Joseph Stalin was an iron-fisted dictator who had "purged"—killed—thousands of opponents in making the Soviet Union into a communist nation. Trusting someone so ruthless was difficult.

But Roosevelt and Churchill knew that they needed Stalin's help. With the Soviets in the war in Europe against Germany, Hitler had to fight on two fronts; while battling the combined armies of the United States, Great Britain, and France in the west, he had to try to stop the advance of Stalin's forces from the east. The need to fight the war on two fronts stretched Hitler's supplies and weakened his forces, and hastened his final defeat.

Even before the war had ended, though, the Western powers knew they had a problem. In advancing on Germany, Soviet troops had swept west-

Stalin, Roosevelt, and Churchill discuss plans for treatment of Germany during World War II. The leaders believed that by working together, they could defeat Nazi Germany.

EUROPE DURING WORLD WAR II

A map of Europe during World War II shows the Soviet Union in relation to Eastern Europe. The United States needed the help of the Soviets to defeat Germany and Japan. Nevertheless, Roosevelt exercised caution when dealing with Stalin, fearing that he might retain Soviet troops in Eastern Europe.

ward through Poland, Austria, Czechoslovakia, and Hungary. Roosevelt and Churchill began to suspect that Stalin might never pull his troops out of these countries. He seemed to be using the approaching end of the war as an excuse to extend Soviet rule over much of Eastern Europe.

The diplomatic situation was a ticklish one. If the United States challenged Stalin, the Soviets might refuse to help in the final defeat of the Nazis and, more importantly, of Japan. Stalin might also refuse to relax his grip in Eastern Europe. But if the United States failed to challenge him, the people of those countries might remain under Soviet domination.

Yalta

In dealing with Stalin, Roosevelt had generally taken the path of cooperation. He had hoped to do so again in February 1945, when he and Churchill met with Stalin at Yalta, a Russian port city on the Black Sea. In a conference that turned out to have major historical importance, the leaders of the "Big Three" powers discussed a number of issues related to the end of the war in Europe. The continent was

Truman and adviser Stimson meet to discuss post-war plans for dealing with the Soviet Union.

in chaos, food was scarce, cities were destroyed, and many people were homeless. Roosevelt hoped that American-Soviet cooperation would benefit the European people. But his major goal was to make sure that as American, British, and French troops withdrew from the war zones, Soviet forces did not move in. He was also concerned about Soviet troop movements in the Far East, especially on the border between the Soviet Union and Manchuria.

The three leaders reached several historic agreements at the Yalta conference that seemed at the time to have achieved Roosevelt's goals for freedom and stability in postwar Europe and Asia. First, they confirmed plans they had already discussed to divide Germany into separate zones that would be occupied by each of the Allies—the United States, Britain, France, and the Soviet Union. Second, they scheduled a meeting to prepare a charter for the new United Nations. Finally, they signed a Declaration on Liberated Europe, affirming "the right of all people to choose the form of government under which they live" through "democratic means" and "free elections." Roosevelt returned from Yalta flush with success. But in the final days of his life, he was beginning to see that the Yalta agreements were not restraining Soviet behavior. It was becoming clear that the United States and the Soviets were headed for their own showdown.

The showdown came in April. The primary issue was Poland. Prior to Yalta, Stalin had established a communist government in Poland that turned Poland into a "puppet" state—one that would bow to Stalin's will. In signing the Yalta Declaration, Stalin seemed to have agreed to allow "free and unfettered" elections in Poland. Like Roosevelt, Truman believed that Stalin was breaking the promises he had made at Yalta and was simply trying to seize territory. Faced with a delicate political situation—an "ally" who was acting more like an enemy—the new president neither avoided the problem nor tried to play the part of the polished diplomat. Instead, in a bitter exchange of words, he told Molotov, Stalin's representative, exactly what he thought.

A War of Words

Many of Truman's advisers, including Stimson and Byrnes, were in favor of the president's tough approach to the Soviets. The feeling was already growing throughout the nation that Roosevelt, in a misguided attempt to get along with the Soviets, had "given away" Eastern and Central Europe by signing agreements that he had no real way of enforcing. Further, he had told Stalin at Yalta—and he has been criticized for decades for saying this—that the American people would not be willing to keep a large army in Europe after the war, an army that would offset Soviet strength. Stalin's refusal to allow free elections in Poland showed that he felt that

"I stood squarely behind all commitments and agreements entered into by our late great president [Roosevelt]."

Pres. Harry S. Truman

"Far from following his predecessor's policy of cooperation . . . Truman launched a powerful foreign policy initiative aimed at reducing or eliminating Soviet influence in Europe."

Gar Alperovitz, historian

The characteristic mushroom cloud rises over Nagasaki.

Roosevelt's "weakness" had given him a free hand, that he could do anything he wanted. So Truman's advisers thought that only an immediate and firm showdown with the Soviets would keep them from taking over most of the region. But at the same time, these advisers were starting to fear that the United States could do little to keep Stalin from having his way. Secretary of State Byrnes later put it this way: "It was not a question of what we would *let* the Russians do, but what we could *get* them to do."

In spite of the tension, the United States and the Soviet Union remained allies during the final defeat of Nazi Germany in May 1945. But underneath the

In early May, Harry Hopkins was sent to foster diplomatic relations with Stalin. Why did Truman keep this meeting a secret?

show of friendship, the alliance between the two nations was breaking up and distrust was building. Some even thought it possible that war could break out between American and Soviet forces in Europe.

Thus, during the spring of 1945, a war in Europe was ending. A war in the Pacific was still raging. And a third war, a "Cold War," was just beginning.

Was the mushroom cloud that rose over Hiroshima not an end, but a beginning? Was the atomic bombing of Japan an attempt by President Truman not to bring about a Japanese surrender, but to control the Soviets?

Secret Mission to Moscow

In early May, Truman seemed suddenly to reverse his course. He called out of retirement one of Roosevelt's most respected diplomats, Harry Hopkins, and sent him on a mission to Moscow. Hopkins's purpose was to discuss the Polish problem with Stalin. What is interesting about the Hopkins mission is that Truman kept it a complete secret, even from such top advisers as his own secretary of state!

The question that every historian of the period has asked is Why? Truman had taken a tough stand in public, but now, by sending Hopkins to meet with Stalin, he seemed to be taking a cooperative, diplomatic stand in private. Was the Hopkins mission intended to smooth over the ill feeling left by the Molotov meeting? Or was this simple haberdasher from Missouri playing a craftier game with Stalin?

Historian Herbert Feis expresses the most widely held view of the Hopkins mission—that Truman was trying to regain the cooperative spirit of the Roosevelt administration. Being a firm negotiator would help Truman politically, but much could be gained by lowering the tension between the two nations. The European people would benefit. The upcoming first meeting of the United

"I am firmly convinced that the Russians will eventually agree to the American proposals for the establishment of an atomic energy authority of world-wide scope, *provided* they are convinced that we would have the bomb in quantity and would use it without hesitation in another war."

James Conant, historian

"I was inclined to think we ought to hang on to the bomb . . . and its secrets; but . . . I had found that I was wrong and that that would be by far the most dangerous course."

Henry Stimson, President Truman's secretary of war

Stalin confers with Soviet foreign minister Vyacheslav M. Molotov. What secrets do they share?

Nations in San Francisco would be more successful. Most important, Stalin would fulfill his promise at Yalta to enter the war against Japan. So it was important to Truman to make some concessions to Stalin. In this way he could win some Soviet concessions that would help the United States.

But this fails to explain why Truman kept the mission a secret. If he had really decided that he needed to keep the goodwill of the Soviets, why did he not just do so with the help of his diplomatic advisers? Why did he seem to be taking two contrary positions, one in public, the other in secret?

The answer may lie with Truman's meeting with Stimson and Groves two days after his heated exchange with Molotov. The president knew that the United States would have difficulty backing up the blunt language he used in his meeting with Molotov. In the language of poker he was fond of using, he was "bluffing." But Stimson, who knew about the secret of the atomic bomb, could see the issue in a different light and concluded that it was time for the president to know that the Manhattan Project would soon pay off. He knew that the bomb would be a master card in American talks with the Soviets. Armed with the most powerful weapon in history, the United States would be better able to influence Soviet actions and block Soviet aggression.

Those who take this view of the Hopkins mission, historians like Gar Alperovitz, Gregg Herkin, and Martin Sherwin, look closely at the sequence of events during these weeks:

April 23: Truman has a stormy meeting with the Soviet foreign minister, who refuses to back down from the president's demands for Soviet restraint in Eastern Europe.

April 24: Stimson asks for a meeting with the president.

April 25: Stimson and Groves inform Truman that the United States will soon have in its arsenal a weapon of unimaginable force.

May 1-8: Truman seems to reverse his position and sends a goodwill ambassador to Moscow.

Stalling for Time

What conclusions can be drawn? One is that after April 25, Truman believed he no longer needed to bluff! He believed that the atomic bomb in American hands would be a threat to the Soviets, making them more cooperative, maybe even getting them out of Eastern Europe. The United States would be able to establish a stable peace in Europe without the need to keep a large army there. Further, Truman began to think that the United States no longer needed Soviet help to win the war against Japan. He began to think that the goal now was to wrap up the Pacific war *before* the Soviets could get in! According to this view, then, the mysterious Hopkins mission was not a retreat. The president was not backing down, nor was he simply trying to lessen tension. What was he doing? He was stalling for time until the bomb could be developed and successfully tested. As he said in May: "We shall probably hold more cards in our hands later than now."

The Bomb as a Diplomatic Threat

Another interesting fact suggests that Truman was eager to use the bomb as a diplomatic threat against the Soviets. As the problems in Europe continued to grow, it became clear that the Western allies had to confront Stalin directly. Time was important, for soon the United States would have to pull its troops out of Europe to fight Japan, leaving Europe defenseless against Soviet aggression. A meeting was arranged, to include once again Churchill, Stalin, and the American president. This time, the site chosen for the confrontation was Potsdam, a city on the outskirts of Berlin.

When the possibility of such a meeting was first discussed, though, the bomb was not yet ready. Although the reports from Los Alamos were optimistic, Truman did not want to risk any embarrassment. He did not want to try to stare down the Soviets until the bomb had been successfully tested. Told that the earliest test date would be in July, Truman *twice* postponed the Potsdam Conference, finally agreeing to a starting date of July 17. He arrived at Potsdam on July 15. On July 16 he received word that the test at Alamogordo had been a success. Stimson's diaries emphasize how bold and confident the president became. In the meetings on July 17 and for the next week, Truman resumed his firm approach toward Stalin, challenging his aggressive actions in Eastern Europe. Had Truman deliberately waited for the atomic bomb test before trying to take on the Soviets again?

If so, why did he continue to say that his "one

President Roosevelt signs a declaration of war against Japan.

THE FAR EAST DURING WORLD WAR II

objective was to be sure to get the Russians into the Japanese war so as to save the lives of 100,000 American boys"?

Trouble Brews in Asia

While tension was mounting over Europe, matters were no better in the Far East. Roosevelt had sought cooperation from the Soviets on two matters and thought he had received it at Yalta. First, he wanted Stalin to promise to enter the war against Japan. Ill feeling between Japan and Russia went back at least to 1904, when Japan attacked Russia and took control of Russian territory. Russians had always wanted revenge, so despite the Soviet-Japanese non-aggression pact, Stalin readily pro-

A map shows Japan in relation to the Soviet Union. In 1904, Japan seized Russian-held territory in Manchuria, accounting for Stalin's willingness to enter the war against Japan.

mised to enter the war in the Pacific after Germany fell. Secondly, Roosevelt wanted Stalin to support a non-communist Chinese government friendly to the United States. In return, Russia would get back the territories Japan seized in the 1904 war. More important, the agreement at Yalta gave the Soviets access to the Manchurian port city of Dairen in northeast China. They would also be allowed to keep a naval base at nearby Port Arthur. (Russia historically has wanted to be able to get to ports like these—warm water ports to the south, where shipping and naval operations can go on year-round.) The Soviets would be able to get to these ports by crossing Manchuria on a railroad line owned jointly by the Soviet Union and China.

Stalin's Motives

Despite these agreements at Yalta, matters in the Far East were becoming tense. Stalin was massing troops on the border between the Soviet Union and Manchuria, a logical place for the Soviets to enter the war against Japan. But by the spring, it seemed apparent that Stalin was not grouping forces solely to help the United States against Japan. He was grabbing for more territory. If he did enter the war, he would be in position to seize Manchuria, dominate all of northern China, control Korea, and demand to be part of an occupation of Japan. As they were in Europe, the stakes were high and time was important. Steps had to be taken to prevent the Soviet "Red Army" from pouring across the border into Manchuria. Secretary Stimson wrote in May, "It may be necessary to have it out with Russia on her relations to Manchuria."

Yet once again, Truman did not act. The usual view is that he did not confront Stalin on these issues because he did not want to increase tension. Relations were strained enough over Europe, and he still wanted the Soviets to enter the war. But another

"Byrnes had already told me . . . that in his belief the bomb might well put us in a position to dictate our own terms at the end of the war."

Pres. Harry S. Truman

"I shared Byrnes's concern about Russia's throwing her weight around in the postwar period, but I was completely flabbergasted by the assumption that rattling the bomb might make Russia more manageable."

Leo Szilard, physicist

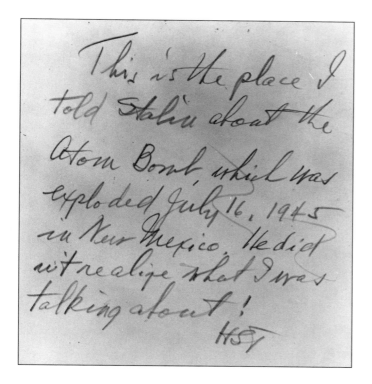

A hand-written note by Truman states that Stalin didn't know about the atomic bomb which was exploded on July 16, 1945. Did Truman drop the bombs on Japan as a spectacular demonstration for the Soviet Union?

view is that he once again was stalling until the atomic bomb was ready. In May the United States could do little to stop a Soviet invasion of Manchuria. The best that could be done was to have the Chinese foreign minister, who was friendly to American interests, carry on long talks with the Soviets about relations with the Chinese government and the details of the Dairen-Port Arthur arrangement. According to this view, held by Alperovitz and others, these talks, combined with the Hopkins mission, were designed to keep the Soviets from taking decisive action in Europe and in the Far East—to stall. But in July, armed with a working bomb, Truman could back up American goals—with deadly force if necessary. Stimson wrote, "Over any such tangled weave of problems [the atomic bomb] secret would be dominant."

Churchill, Truman, and Stalin
are all smiles as they shake
hands. Underneath the show
of friendship, did Truman
believe that Stalin was trying
to seize territory?

Thus, if this theory is correct, Truman's overall strategy was to use the bomb to make Stalin more manageable in Europe and the Far East. These interpretations of Truman's actions are just theories. Little direct evidence proves what Truman was thinking during these weeks. He continued to say that the atomic bomb was a way to end the war quickly and save American lives. Many of his closest advisers, though, including James Byrnes, were arguing that the bomb's greatest usefulness was as a threat against the Soviets.

Direct evidence does exist, however, of Truman's thinking while he was in Potsdam. During the days he was there, the president made a number of entries in a journal that was found in 1979. Also, letters he wrote to his wife, Bess, from Potsdam turned up four years later in a collection of her papers. The importance of these documents is that they provide the only direct view of Truman's thinking at the time. They give, in his own hand, a glimpse of a still-new president struggling with the question of how to use a new force to reach American goals. But they are filled with contradictions, and they raise as many questions as they answer.

Did Truman Have Ulterior Motives?

On the evening of June 16, for example, just hours after he had learned of the successful test of the atomic bomb, Truman wrote in his journal, "It seems the most terrible thing ever discovered, but it can be made the most useful." This seems like a simple statement—that the bomb would force a Japanese surrender, end the war, and end the need for an American invasion of Japan. Is it possible, though, that Truman was thinking that the weapon would be "useful" as a threat against the Soviets in the days ahead?

The Potsdam Conference began the next day, and the new president met with Stalin for the first time. That evening Truman wrote in his journal, "I have some dynamite, too, which I'm not exploding

Truman, Churchill, and Stalin are photographed at the Potsdam Conference in June 1945.

Truman and his wife wave from the platform of a train. Will anyone ever know Truman's real motives for bombing Japan?

now." Again, his statement is open to two interpretations. Was he referring simply to one of his conference proposals? Or was he referring to the atomic bomb, which he believed Stalin knew nothing about?

Truman also wrote that he received that day a pledge from Stalin to enter the war against Japan: "He'll be in the Jap War on August 15. . . . Fini Japs when that comes about." Then on July 18, he wrote Mrs. Truman:

> I've gotten what I came for—Stalin goes to war on August 15 with no strings on it. . . . I'll say that we'll end the war a year sooner now, and think of the kids who won't be killed! That is the important thing.

Journal Entries Raise Questions

What was Truman really saying in these passages? That the combined might of the United States and the Soviet Union would easily defeat Japan? Or that a Soviet declaration of war on August 15 would persuade Japan to surrender? Either way, Truman's comments raise another important question: If Soviet entry in the war would hasten its end, why did Truman, just a week later, order that the bombs be dropped as early as possible in August?

Truman's thinking gets even harder to follow. He wrote in his journal on July 18:

> [Churchill] and I ate alone. Discussed Manhattan (it is a success). Decided to tell Stalin about it. Stalin had told [Churchill] of telegram from Jap emperor asking for peace. Stalin also read his answer to me. It was satisfactory. [I] believe Japs will fold up before Russia comes in. I am sure they will when Manhattan appears over their homeland. I shall inform Stalin about it at an opportune time.

Here, Truman says that he "believes" Japan will surrender before the Soviets declare war on August

15. He "knows," though, that they will when the bomb is dropped. He seems to be saying that Soviet help against Japan was not needed. Why, then, did he write to his wife, "I've gotten what I came for—Stalin goes to war"? Why did he write on July 20, "I want the Jap War won and I want 'em both [Churchill and Stalin] in it"?

The journal entries raise another question: What would be the "opportune time" for Truman to tell Stalin about the atomic bomb? Truman actually said very little about it to Stalin. He made a casual comment about a "new weapon," but added no details. To the disappointment of the American delegation, Stalin showed little interest. Why did Truman not lay his master card on the table for Stalin to see? Was he still afraid that the bomb would not live up to its promise? Or was he afraid that if Stalin knew the details, he would rush Soviet entry into Manchuria, fearing the war would end before he could capture any territory?

Or was the "opportune time" August 6, when Stalin could see the bomb's terrifying results?

Time has placed before us the possibility that the atomic bombing of Hiroshima and Nagasaki was not a necessary act of war. According to this view, the bombs were not used to end the war, to save American lives, to force a Japanese surrender, or to keep Soviet forces from invading China. According to this view, they were a way to get the world, but especially the Soviets, to accept American goals in Europe and the Far East. Truman dropped the bombs, according to this view, to demonstrate that the United States had the ultimate diplomatic weapon.

Six

Will We Ever Know the Real Reasons?

(opposite page) A soldier stands in a sea of rubble before a building that was once a movie house in bombed-out Hiroshima.

The atomic bombing of Hiroshima might well be the single most important historical event of the twentieth century. It has inspired poets and artists. It has intrigued military historians, who want to know if it was necessary; philosophers, who want to know if it was right; and people the world over, who want to know if it could ever happen again. Harry Truman has been praised as the president willing to make the tough call, and he has been condemned as the president guilty of an atrocity. Viewpoints differ, but no one denies that the rubble of Hiroshima and Nagasaki marked a basic change in the nature of war. Never again would the armies of the world's nations meet in battle without the possibility of nuclear weapons destroying civilization. And in a world where that danger always exists, the shadow of Hiroshima has changed what is meant by the phrase "being at peace."

People seek explanations for events that are so far-reaching in their consequences. Historians examine the records, searching for clues that will explain these events, the reasons they happened, and the states of mind of the people who set them in motion. But in the process of explaining, it is almost impossible to avoid judging. Truman, like all

Emperor Hirohito of Japan saluting prior to naval maneuvers in the Pacific.

presidents before and after him, made a decision that put him on trial in the court of public opinion.

Those who condemn his decision are likely to do so for one of two major reasons:

1. Truman was not truthful with the public, perhaps not even with himself. Knowing full well that an invasion of Japan was not needed and that Japan was about to surrender, he ordered that the bombs be dropped.

2. Truman was afraid. Sensing that America's power in the postwar world was being challenged by the Soviets, he used the bomb as a brutish display of force.

But here is the other side of the ledger:

1. The president had an obligation to use any means at hand to end a long, costly war in which thousands of Americans had been killed.

2. Japan was an enemy not to be trusted. The treachery of the Japanese attack on a sleeping Pearl Harbor in 1941 was still an open wound to many Americans. At any moment the factions that favored war could have seized power in Japan and found some way to launch another attack.

3. The atomic bomb was a totally new weapon. Truman did not fully appreciate its power. In later years atomic and nuclear weapons acquired the ability to frighten people by their numbers. But in 1945, there were only two, and they were just another weapon. Once the bombs were dropped and Truman had a clearer sense of how terrifying they are, he ordered that the bombing be stopped. Truman should not be condemned for using a weapon he could not have understood.

4. By the time Truman made his decision, the twentieth century had changed the way leaders thought about war and how it should be conducted. The firebombings of Dresden, Germany, and Tokyo, Japan, randomly killed tens of thousands of civilians. Condemning Truman for continuing that strategy by bombing Hiroshima and Nagasaki is unfair.

What was President Truman's "real reason" for ordering the atomic bombing of Hiroshima and Nagasaki? The question suggests that he had a single, compelling motive. In reality, though, historians may never agree on a single motive. The president was caught in a complicated web of military, diplomatic, and political concerns. The pressures of the time were no doubt pushing him in different directions at the same time. His decision to use the bomb is one more example of humanity's effort to balance the conflicting demands of human emotion and sober logic.

Was it necessary for Truman to drop this instrument of tremendous destruction on Japan?

The Danger of a Genie

An image that is often used to describe atomic weapons is that they are like a genie in a bottle. As long as the lid is kept on, the genie will stay inside and do no harm. Once the lid is taken off, the genie can escape, and it might be impossible to get it back in.

The genie peeked out of the bottle in August 1945. It was put back in then, and since that time, no nuclear weapon has been used in war. To keep the genie in the bottle, it is necessary to go back to the start of the atomic age and ask the kinds of questions raised in this book. By knowing how the genie escaped once, perhaps future leaders can make sure that it never happens again.

Postscript

The story of Japan's internal political struggle continued even after the Nagasaki bombing. On August 8, the Soviet Union finally dashed the militarists' hopes by declaring war on Japan. On the tenth, Japan offered to surrender, again on the condition that its government be kept and that Hirohito be allowed to remain as emperor.

But many Americans still urged the president to reject the Japanese surrender offer. Truman sent a message to the Japanese that simply did not respond to the condition they had offered.

The reaction to Truman's message in Japan was almost a disaster. The moderate factions, who were looking for peace, quickly lost power. The militarists became bolder and nearly staged a successful military takeover of the government. Their attempt failed only because the war minister did not give them his support. If he had, the takeover would probably have succeeded. In that case, Japan would probably not have surrendered on August 14. The war would have been prolonged.

A third atomic bomb was being assembled. Its target was Tokyo. Fortunately, it was never dropped.

Emperor Hirohito remained on the throne until his death in January 1989.

(opposite page) The Trinity Site Memorial stands in New Mexico, at the site of the first atomic bomb detonation.

For Further Exploration

Michael O'Neal particularly recommends the following books and articles for young readers interested in learning more about the decision to drop the atomic bombs on Japan.

Books

Paul R. Baker, ed., *The Atomic Bomb: The Great Decision*. New York: Holt, Rinehart & Winston, 1968.

Arthur H. Compton, *Atomic Quest: A Personal Narrative*. New York: Oxford University Press, 1956.

Herbert Feis, *The Atomic Bomb and the End of World War II*. Princeton, NJ: Princeton University Press, 1966.

Robert H. Ferrell, ed., *Dear Bess: The Letters from Harry to Bess Truman, 1910-1959*. New York: Norton, 1983.

Robert H. Ferrel, *Off the Record: The Private Papers of Harry S. Truman*. New York: Harper & Row, 1980.

Harry S. Truman, *Memoirs: Year of Decisions*. New York: Doubleday, 1955.

Articles

Barton J. Bernstein, "The Dropping of the A-Bomb," *The Center Magazine*, March/April, 1983.

Walter Isaacson, "Why Did We Drop the Bomb?" *Time*, August 19, 1985.

P. M. Jones, "Three Great Decisions: What Would You Have Done?" *Scholastic Update*, February 26, 1988.

Samuel Eliot Morrison, "Why Japan Surrendered," *The Atlantic Monthly*, October 1960.

Henry Stimson, "The Decision to Use the Atomic Bomb," *Harper's Magazine,* February 1947.

Works Consulted

Books

Gar Alperovitz, *Atomic Diplomacy*. New York: Simon & Schuster, 1965.

P. M. S. Blackett, *Fear, War, and the Bomb*. New York: Whittlesey House, 1948.

Gregg Herken, *The Winning Weapon: The Atomic Bomb and the Cold War,* 1945-1950. New York: Knopf, 1981.

Martin J. Sherwin, *A World Destroyed: The Atomic Bomb and the Grand Alliance*. New York: Knopf, 1975.

Articles

Gar Alperovitz, "More on Atomic Diplomacy," *Bulletin of the Atomic Scientists*, December 1985.

Barton J. Bernstein, "The Perils and Politics of Surrender," *Pacific Historical Review*, February 1977.

Barton J. Bernstein, "A Postwar Myth: 500,000 U.S. Lives Saved," *Bulletin of the Atomic Scientists*, June-July 1986.

Kai Erikson, "Of Accidental Judgments and Casual Slaughters," *The Nation*, August 3-10, 1985.

Robert L. Messer, "New Evidence on Truman's Decision," *Bulletin of the Atomic Scientists*, August 1985.

Martin J. Sherwin, "How Well They Meant," *Bulletin of the Atomic Scientists*, August 1985.

Index

Picture Credits

Acme Newsphotos, courtesy National Archives, 92
Acme Newsphotos, courtesy Harry S. Truman Library, 86
AP/Wide World Photos, 18, 20, 43, 63, 84, 101
Consulate General of Japan, N.Y., 78
Courtesy Dwight D. Eisenhower Library, 74
Harris & Ewing, courtesy Harry S. Truman Library, 36
Los Alamos National Laboratory, 21, 25(bottom), 70, 77(both), 103, 105
Los Alamos Scientific Laboratory, 25(top), 83
National Archives, 22, 33, 35, 39, 40, 49, 50, 51, 64, 68, 88, 90
National Park Services/Abbie Rowe, courtesy Harry S. Truman Library, 23, 98
Naval Photographic Center, 80
Official A.A.F. Photograph, 79
Smithsonian Institution, 11, 13, 14, 17, 26, 27, 31, 34, 44, 47, 48, 54, 57, 58, 71, 87
U.S. Army, courtesy Harry S. Truman Library, 12, 37, 95, 96, 97
U.S. Marine Corps Photo/Collection of W.H. Christenson, 41
UPI/Bettmann Newsphotos, 53, 55, 59, 60, 69, 72, 73, 75, 76, 102

About the Author

Michael J. O'Neal was born in Elyria, Ohio, in 1949. While he was an undergraduate English major at Bowling Green University, he developed a strong interest in books and writing. He served in the armed forces and then returned to Bowling Green to earn his doctorate. Currently, Michael is a teacher of English at Kirkwood Community College in Cedar Rapids, Iowa. He lives in Iowa City with his wife and children.